Wildlife Mysteries

Raymond P. Holden

WILDLIFE MYSTERIES

Illustrated by Sherry Streeter

DODD, MEAD & COMPANY
New York

ISBN: 0-396-06511-2
Library of Congress Catalog Card Number: 72-720
Printed in the United States of America

Acknowledgments

I SHOULD like to express my thanks to Dr. Clarence Cottam, Director of the Welder Wildlife Foundation, for his kindness in giving me time and place in which to write a great part of this book. I am also grateful to the Richards Free Library, Newport, New Hampshire, for freely given assistance, as I am also indebted to the New Hampshire State Library.

Introduction

A WORD ABOUT MYSTERY

A MYSTERY IS, in the commonest sense, something which is unknown and may appear to be unknowable. Yet many things which at some time in the past may have seemed to be beyond man's ability to discover and understand—the mystery of the other side of the moon, for instance—have been discovered and made, if not commonplace, at least understandable. I like to think of a mystery (and that is how I have used the word in this book) as something which, even when solved, has about it an atmosphere of wonder, a sense, perhaps, of the miraculous. The discovery of the true identity of the honey ant, of the incredible facts of the life history of the lamprey, of the wolf's ability to survive unnoticed in a civilization which denies his existence, does not remove from the honey ant, lamprey, or wolf a sense of wonder. It is truly a miracle that nature has contrived so many ways of arranging for the survival of life, ways which man himself could never have conceived and which, with all his intellectual ingenuity, he could not have devised.

About the fringes of our lives are, merely because we are unaware of them, countless wonders, countless mysteries. Some of us, perhaps, would consider it a bother to have to dig into them, but many of us would like to know more about them. It is exciting to know that life, as in the spider, can persist under almost unbelievable conditions; that unknown animals such as the okapi can exist under our very noses unobserved and undescribed; that evidences of what we believe to be the beauty of nature are really intricate and elaborate arrangements for the transmission of energy from one living thing to another for the continuation of life on earth.

The stories told here are mysteries in one sense or another, although not always unsolved, and there is, I hope, an over-all mystery about them in the fact that they will not all mean the same thing to everyone. I hope, too, that they may help to stimulate in growing men and women a fondness for, rather than a fear of, the unknown and the mysterious.

Contents

1.

The Pygmies' Secret

AFRICA—Central Africa at least—was, in the nineteenth century, a land of many darknesses and legendary wonders. Until David Livingstone's journeys from the 1850's on, the interior was practically unknown. Many of its own tribes knew of each other only by hearsay. Some were fiercely hostile and others were friendly and peaceful. European nations, anxious to take possession of the rich products of the jungle and the plains, moved in. They did not trouble to ask who were the rightful owners of the lands they occupied. They established colonies wherever they wished. Sometimes they fought among themselves, as well as with the native owners, over boundaries which had no real meaning beyond their claims.

Even after Livingstone's tragic death, the region between the Congo and the great Rift Valley which divides the tropical rain forest from the eastern plains remained a deep mystery. Hunters and travelers mistakenly believed that they had identified all the larger animals of the region. They had, in fact, started some of them toward extinction.

During the latter part of the nineteenth century, the Belgians came in and established an organized colony known as the Belgian Congo which provided their nation with both ivory and rubber. Posts were established as far east as the Ituri and Semliki Rivers, but the outside world got very little in the way of news of what went on in the depths of the jungle. Perhaps this was because the Belgian authorities did not wish the world to know how the natives, the rightful owners of the region, were treated.

In the 1860's, Harry Johnston was an inquisitive boy in England. As a child he read a book of tales, partly true and partly fanciful, about strange unknown beasts to be found in Central Africa. One of these was the gorilla, which had been somewhat fantastically described by Paul Du Chaillu, who had run across it in the mountains of Central Africa.

Young Johnston never forgot what he read. What he read stimulated his imagination to the point at which he was almost ready to believe in such a mythical creature as the unicorn. He was particularly impressed by a mention, in Henry M. Stanley's *In Darkest Africa*, of a strange horse or asslike animal which the pygmies of the eastern Congo forest occasionally caught in pitfalls. The unicorn was supposed to be a horse with a single long horn growing from its forehead.

Johnston was interested in what Stanley said, but he could not understand why any relative of the horse, zebra, or wild ass would live in such a deep forest as that in which he knew the pygmies lived. In the Ituri forest it rains most of the time and the sun never reaches the forest floor. There is no suitable grass for horse or cattle, only leafmold and muck.

Perhaps because of his boyhood interest in Africa, Johnston

grew up to become a British civil servant assigned to the colony of Uganda, east of the Belgian Congo. He was eventually knighted for his services to the Crown.

In 1899, Sir Harry was asked by the Belgian authorities to look for and, if possible, recover a group of some twenty-five pygmies who had been kidnapped by a German and taken by their captor into British territory. The ruthless German, who was something like a circus scout, had the idea that the pygmies, who had themselves only recently emerged from the darkness of mystery, would make a decided hit at the great Paris Exposition of 1900. Johnston was glad that the Belgians, whose dealings with natives were

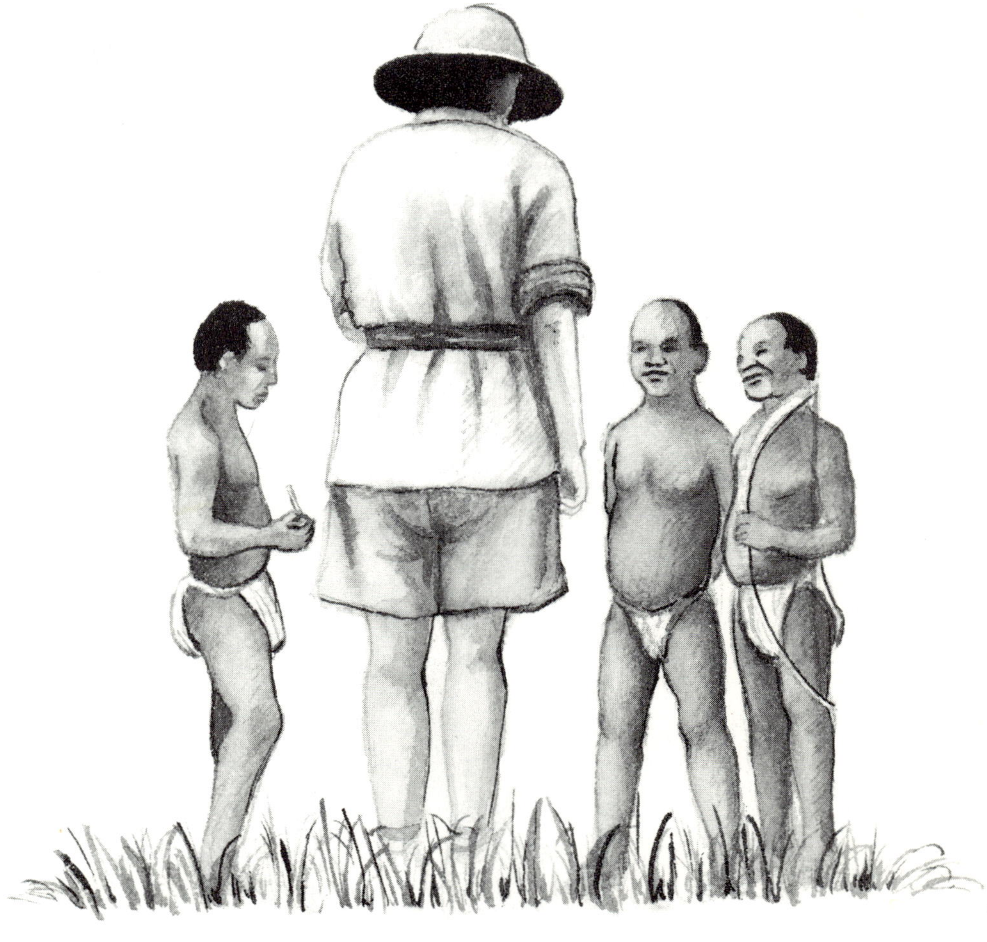

sometimes questionable, did not sympathize with the German's plans. Johnston promptly got together a small expedition and set out in search of the German and his captives. These were located without any great difficulty. The German, who for political reasons could not be severely punished, was sent back to Germany. The pygmies became Harry Johnston's wards. It was his duty to return them to their homes. The Belgians had asked him to do so.

Johnston was as interested in rare people as he was in rare animals. The pygmies were rare people indeed. They were forest folk who lived in the Ituri-Semliki region of the northeastern Belgian Congo. They were only about four feet tall, often less, and they lived almost entirely by hunting with the bow and arrow. Clothes, in their climate, would have been a dreadful bother so they wore none except such G strings, loincloths, and ornaments as satisfied their primitive modesty and pride.

Johnston found them friendly and likable. It saddened him to think what would have happened to the kidnapped group if they had ever been forced to put themselves on display at the Paris Exposition.

Sir Harry enjoyed the difficult trip across the Semliki River and spent most of his time endearing himself to his wards, who had been thoroughly frightened by their narrow escape. He asked many questions about the great forest to the west and managed somehow to understand most of the answers. One of his questions was about the horselike animal mentioned by Henry M. Stanley. Scientists and the unscientific press had speculated about this and made varying guesses as to what it might be—guesses ranging from a zebra to a unicorn, which was by that time discredited as a genuine animal. As the pygmies, who said they knew the creature well, described it, the animal did sound like a zebra. Primitive people like the pygmies have a way of telling a white man what they think he wants to hear.

When Johnston and his safari reached the first Belgian post in the Congo he told the Belgian officers what the pygmies had said. The officers claimed that they were well acquainted with the beast although, since they had never seen a living specimen, it did not seem to have occurred to them to wonder what it really was. They said that the natives often brought the "unknown" animal in as food and that the pygmies and non-pygmy blacks made belts and bandoliers (for carrying arrows or ammunition) out of the skin of its legs, which were striped horizontally in irregular bands of dark brown and white. The natives and the Belgian soldiers described the animal as a horselike creature with great ears, a narrow nose, and more than one hoof on each foot. They were not animal experts and mystery did not seem to concern them.

Johnston knew he was on the track of something remarkable. In spite of his misgivings about its habitat, he thought it might be the *Hipparion*, a supposedly extinct three-toed horse. Johnston and his staff searched the deep forest but found no trace of such a creature. The natives pointed out tracks, which the Englishman followed. As these were the tracks of a cloven-hoofed animal, not one with more than one hoof to a foot, Johnston began to think he was being deceived—in ignorance rather than intentionally. He decided that the mysterious creature must be a forest antelope of some sort rather than a horse. Nevertheless, he would have kept up his search but for the fact that the heat and humidity were becoming too much for his party. All of the Europeans except Johnston himself and all of the native bearers and guides came down with fever. Johnston knew that it was necessary to return to the high grasslands. He was disappointed that all he could take with him was a few small samples of skin which did not prove that the pygmies' secret was not a zebra. His one hope was that one of the Belgian officers would make good his promise to send Johnston a whole skin, perhaps even a skeleton.

In the meantime, Sir Harry shipped what fragments of pelt he had to London, together with the information that the natives called it something which sounded like "okapi."

The fragments were examined at the British Museum and were publicly described by the well-known scientist P. L. Sclater as *Equus johnstoni* or "Johnston's horse." There was nothing world-shaking in that.

While the discovery of a new type of horse, or zebra, was being announced in London, Johnston received from Karl Eriksson, a Swede in the service of the Belgian Congo administration, a complete skin and skull from a freshly killed okapi. While it was difficult to make any positive identification without the soft parts of the body and the hooves, which were also missing, Johnston finally realized that what he had was no horse. He felt certain, although its form was like nothing ever seen before, that the creature was related to the giraffe. He knew that a certain primitive ancestor of the giraffe, believed extinct, had lived millions of years ago in Greece, Asia Minor, and India. This animal, called *Halladotherium*, was known only from fossil specimens. It was somewhat larger and had a longer neck than the new okapi. Nevertheless Johnston, for a time, referred to his find as *Halladotherium.*

Harry Johnston sent his new complete skin and skull, together with what information he had, to London, where it came into the hands of a man who recognized it for what it was—a completely unknown animal. Sir E. Ray Lankester reported the find to the International Zoological Congress at Berlin in 1901. He established the fact that it belonged to a new branch of the giraffe family. The name *Okapia johnstoni* was suggested and confirmed.

The world was astonished to find that a completely strange beast of such large size could have existed for years in the Congo forest without making itself known. Scientists very often declare the existence of a new variety, species or subspecies, because they have discovered a slight difference in bony structure or color or shape of internal organs which the layman would not notice at all. This was not the case with the okapi, which not even the layman could think looked like anything ever seen before. It had no real resemblance to the great giraffe of the African plains, nor, in spite of its stripes, did it look at all like a zebra. Johnston's okapi stands between the present giraffe of Africa and the extinct upper-Miocene (the name given to a geological time dating back many million years) *Samotherium.* It is also related to the extinct *Paleotragus* of southern Europe and Persia.

The okapi remains rare not particularly because of scarcity so much as by reason of the difficulty of capturing him. Most large

museums now have mounted specimens and some zoological parks have or have had live ones. A live okapi was exhibited at the Bronx Zoo in New York in 1937. Yet the strange creature lives a shy and secluded life in a jungle world which cannot be imagined by anyone who has not visited it. It is a region of tall trees and low undergrowth in which the humidity is always extremely high and the temperature hangs around 100 degrees day and night. The undergrowth is made up of many broad-leaved plants which grow taller than a man and whose leaves, constantly wet, reflect a striped radiance along their veins. With this background the okapi's dark brown, glossy coat and white striped fore and hind legs and haunches blend beautifully.

The okapi which, unlike the giraffe, has fore and hind legs of almost equal length, does not really run but ambles like a camel. When in motion its head is kept lowered, its enormous ears raised, its long, narrow, and flexible lips ready to seize upon leaves and flowering plants, or, when the animal pauses, to snuffle and suck at the boggy soil. Its sense of smell is not very keen but its ears are amazingly sharp to catch the slightest sound. So acute is the okapi's hearing that even the barefoot, silent pygmies are seldom able to approach it. As the animal cannot be distinguished in the jungle at a greater distance than twenty-five yards, it is not strange that it is rarely seen. It is probable that the okapi does not know that he has been discovered and that millions of people do not know that he was ever unknown.

It is to be hoped that the okapi's keen hearing and protective coloration will enable him to survive in his dark forest home, lighted only by raindrops and the blooms of orchids and other jungle plants. The threat of the white man's firearms and the need of the native peoples of Africa for more living room may not allow him to remain a mystery.

2.

The Quest for the Honey Ant

IT HAS LONG been known that there are ants which are good, or comparatively good, to eat, some tasting like raspberries and others like honey. The Indians of northern Mexico have served bowlsful of so-called honey ants as delicacies at wedding feasts for centuries. This hospitable practice was not widely known, however, until 1832 when Pablo de Llave wrote an article in a small Mexican scientific magazine describing the custom more thoroughly than he described the ant which made it possible. From Llave's account no one could tell what sort of ant it was that was so esteemed by wedding guests. As a matter of fact, he had never seen a living specimen of it.

It was many years before this remarkable and mysterious source of sweet was written about by anyone who knew of it by anything more than hearsay. Unfortunately, even the first writers who had actually seen a honey ant were not very careful observers, nor were they able to write accurately about what they observed.

Dr. Henry Christopher McCook, a remarkably gifted Philadelphia clergyman who had time and the right kind of mind to double as a scientist, was forty-two years old in 1879. It disturbed

Dr. McCook very much to discover that nearly fifty years after the first report of what had come to be known as honey ants their exact nature was still a mystery. Apparently no one had taken the trouble to locate and dig up and give an accurate description of this ant and its nest.

McCook thought this state of affairs a rather black mark on the face of natural science in America and he determined to clean up the blotch. With the help of the Academy of Natural Sciences of Philadelphia, he got together the proper equipment and camp gear. He and a couple of young assistants then set out on an expedition in search of the truth about the mysterious *Myrmecocystus* —or ant with a bladder—which was its scientific name.

Dr. McCook went directly to Santa Fe, New Mexico, where *Myrmecocystus* had been somewhat vaguely reported by several travelers. McCook knew that the ants were there and he had the time, the equipment, the patience, and the scientific discipline to find *Myrmecocystus*, if he was lucky. He hoped to come back with a complete life history and explanation of the creature's strange but very successful honey production.

The task did not prove easy. It was as if the inquisitive clergyman had gone to a library to look up a book which he knew was there, confident that he would return with the knowledge which the book contained. Unfortunately, in the library of the high New Mexican valley, dotted with piñon, cactus, and rabbit brush, dry (in July) and stony, there was no librarian and no card catalog. There were, too, things about the habits of *Myrmecocystus* which made the ants unavailable at the time when nature's library might have been expected to be open. Although Dr. McCook did not know it at the time, the honey ants never emerge from their nests in daylight.

McCook set up his camp and began his search. For days, handicapped by the vagueness of earlier reporters, he had no luck. There were plenty of ants about but none which even remotely resembled the currant-shaped, pea-sized *Myrmecocystus.* Somewhat discouraged, he decided to pay a visit to his friend, General Charles Adams, Indian fighter and lover of the West who lived at Manitou, Colorado, some 250 miles to the north of Santa Fe, in the shadow of Pikes Peak. General Adams' house was outside of Manitou in the mouth of a high valley between two pincerlike ridges, known as the Garden of the Gods. The area was filled with wind-carved, red sandstone monuments supposed to resemble the gods of the ancient world.

Dr. McCook, even on a nonscientific visit, could not, in walking about with his host, keep his eyes off the ground. There always might be an ant which he had never seen before. In the Garden of the Gods there was.

McCook knew ant hills and ant nests better than most Americans of his time. Yet he did not recognize the little gravelly volcano, not more than three or four inches high, which spread its flat crater almost beneath his feet. He stopped short, aware that here was the entrance to the home of a colony of ants entirely new to him. McCook was not thinking of honey ants. No one had yet reported a sight of them north of New Mexico and very few had been found north of Old Mexico. A new ant is a new ant, however.

Dr. McCook cut a straw from the pale dry grama grass which grew in patches among the red and white rocks and inserted it into the entrance hole of the nest. This seemed to him to be wider than necessary for the admittance of an ant. He managed to get the colony's sentries sufficiently aroused to attack and cling to the straw and so be brought out into daylight. As McCook had never seen a honey ant and had only had them described to him, he could do no more than say that these guardians of the nest resembled what he thought he knew of *Myrmecocystus*.

McCook's feeling about his discovery was a combination of the scientific and the religious, the former arousing curiosity, a desire to know, and the latter inspiring his curiosity with a reverent love which colored and sharpened his understanding.

He began digging into the little crater of gravel with his knife. As the entrance led down into the sandstone rock, the digging soon became difficult. McCook found that the tube of the funnel, of which the small gravel heap above the ground was the bowl, led straight down for a few inches and then leveled out into a passageway. This corridor, between one-half and three-quarters of an inch in diameter, tunneled through the rock by ants, seemed to be what Dr. McCook called a vestibule. From it several other passages led off in different directions, some rising toward the gravel mound of the nest entrance and others leading downward.

Because the ant city had been hollowed out from rock rather than soft dry earth, the shapes and contours of passages and chambers were easily noted. Dr. McCook soon found, however, that he had to abandon his penknife and acquire hammers and chisels and a man to help him.

It took him more than three days, sometimes stopping for measurements, sketches, and plaster casts, to uncover all of the thirty-six cubic feet of rock through which the tunnels and chambers had been carried out grain by grain by the tiny ants which inhabited them. Yet the industry and perseverance of the creatures was not what most excited him.

The first real thrill came when the chisel, which had been excavating a long gallery, inch by inch, slipped through into a larger opening. At this point the passageway widened into a chamber. As the excavator leaned down and peered into the impressive but diminutive darkness of this room, it appeared to be about six inches long, four inches wide, and perhaps an inch and a half from floor to ceiling. There was indeed a domed ceiling, but it was not of bare rock. From it hung, like bats in a larger cave, a closely gathered collection of amber-yellow spheres the size of large peas. These curious objects began to stir as the unaccustomed light and the alarming sound of hammer blows approached them.

To Dr. McCook's keen mind there was no mistaking what these strange golden insect lanterns which hung from the roughened ceiling must be. Three sizes of ants had been encountered in the course of the outer excavation. These were the three worker castes: the majors, the minors, and the minims (or *very* small). Between the hanging globes and the roof, now partially exposed to the light,

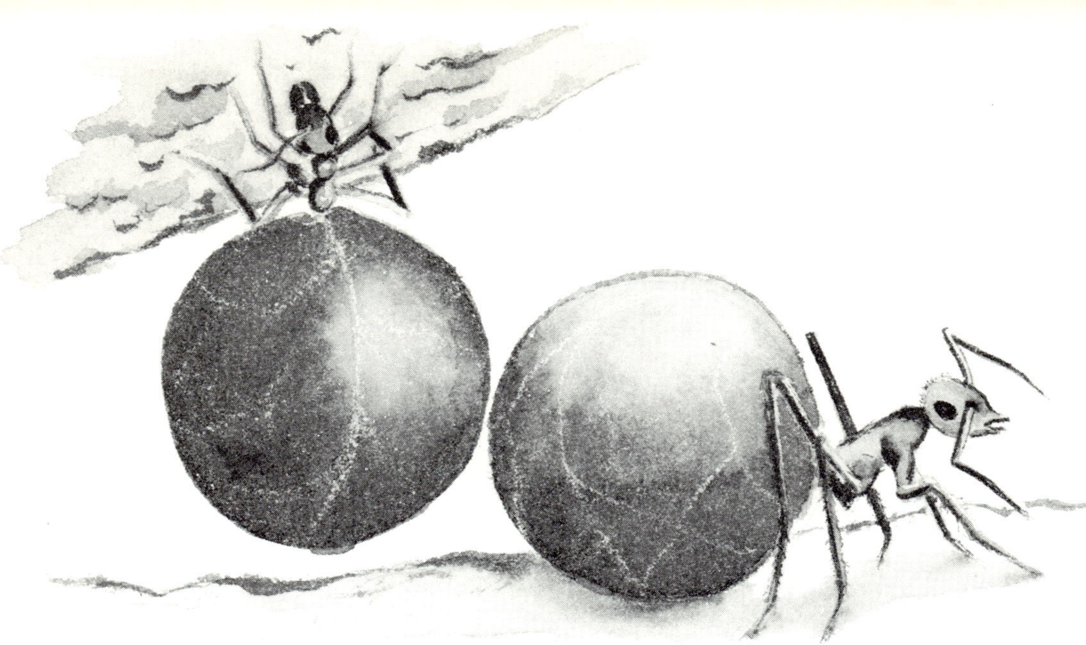

Dr. McCook could see the foreparts of ants like those workers which had been scurrying frantically about in the upper passages. However, only the foreparts, which clung with their legs to the rough roof of the chamber, resembled ants. The abdomens had been transferred into what looked like a tightly packed mass of hairless, honey-colored gooseberries. These were the "rotunds" (meaning, of course, round) or as scientists of today prefer to call them, "repletes" (meaning full). These were the delicacies traditionally served at Mexican weddings.

Tingling with excitement as Dr. McCook was, he realized that, so far, all he had done was to rediscover, in a new locality, an ant already known to exist but never completely and accurately described. True, he had carefully opened and studied the nest and would be able to report on it as no one had yet done. That part of the *Myrmecocystus* puzzle was cleared up.

The main problem, however, was as yet unsolved. It was divided into several questions. First of all, what were the repletes full of? Second, where did they get whatever delicious substance their stuffing might turn out to be? Third, and most interesting of all, were these repletes a fourth caste in the *Myrmecocystus* colony, or were they just ordinary workers who, like ordinary fat men and women, developed a taste for overeating and its consequences?

Dr. McCook resolved to answer these questions. He knew that since Mexicans enjoyed popping the *Myrmecocystus* repletes into their mouths, the inflation of the ants must be the result of absorbing or producing some kind of honeydew. He did not believe that the repletes manufactured honey as bees do, even if the major, minor, and minim workers brought them pollen. Assuming that the contents of the swollen abdomens was a form of honey, its presence within them suggested aphids (sometimes known as plant lice) which are known to secrete droplets of a honeylike substance so that some varieties of ants herd them like cows. No one had ever seen a *Myrmecocystus* milking an aphid—in fact, no one was known to have seen the ant feeding on anything since, as Dr. McCook now realized, they fed only at night. The first thing the doctor did, after gathering a few repletes for study, was to search the vicinity for aphids. He found none, even on the wild roses which were fairly common.

The next step was to shadow the *Myrmecocystus* workers after dark and find out where they went and what they ate. McCook chose an unexcavated ant nest near the tent in which he had been making his headquarters.

On July 27, 1879, at about 7:30 in the evening, the still snowy summit of Pikes Peak glowed rose in the fading light. The red rocks of the Garden of the Gods began to be drowned in a rising tide of blackish-purple shadow. A breeze ruffled the clumps of grama grass and shook the leaves of the shin oaks which grew in thickets between the gullied ridges.

The light from a lantern in the tent cast a dim glow over the area of grass and stones in which the ant hill raised its gravelled crater. Dr. McCook and his helper lay with their heads as near the nest entrance as they could get without frightening any ants which might come up to look about.

Just before dark a few scouts appeared in the funnel-like bowl of the nest, waving their antennae, advancing a few paces and then pausing when they reached the edge. Suddenly a horde of workers rising from the central entrance filled the hollow of the crater. One single ant climbed down the slope of the gravel mound and began to move rapidly northward. This seemed to be the signal for a general advance. Soon a dense, yellowish-brown column was streaming toward an oak thicket some fifty feet from the nest.

Dr. McCook got to his feet and, with the tent lantern, followed the column. In the oak copse the moving formation of ants disintegrated and its members went off in several different directions. Some individuals were picked up by the light of the lantern in a small bush. They seemed to be searching for something but it was impossible to tell what it was. Whatever it might be, they did not seem to find it.

On the next night, at the same hour, McCook took up his watch again, with the same result. It rained hard on the following afternoon and the ground was springy and damp when, for the third time, just before dark, the ants again appeared in parade formation. This time they moved more slowly, perhaps because the rain had weakened the scent of the track and it was more difficult for them to follow it. They seemed to have no recognized leader. Sometimes a tiny minim was out in front, sometimes a minor or a major.

It took the honey ant army seventeen minutes to reach the dense oak thicket where they again disbanded and worked as individuals. By lantern light, maintained with great difficulty since the holder of the light had to keep back the foliage with one hand while clutching the lantern with the other, Dr. McCook tried to follow the ants. It took him a full three hours of exasperating searching before he found a small oak upon which a number of *Myrmecocystus* were crawling, working their way out toward the end of a branch.

It was a struggle to hold the lantern high enough so that its light would not get between his eyes and the object of his search. With only five fingers, it was almost impossible to hold fifteen or twenty twigs which kept snapping back, blocking his view. McCook was nevertheless finally able to make sure that the secret of the honey ants' treasure was before him. The ants were timid, however, and, as had happened on the previous nights, would certainly have given up their activities and disappeared at any sudden commotion among the branches or any unaccustomed sound.

Dr. McCook spent many minutes gaining a few feet so that he might be able to be sure of what he was seeing. When he had got himself, the branches, and his lantern into some sort of balance, he concentrated his attention on the top of the branch toward which he had seen the worker ants making their way. He soon saw what they were doing.

Near the end of each twig, encircling the tiny stems, was a cluster of brown oak galls, which are swellings caused by the attempt of the tree to overcome an injury resulting from a puncture by a fly. This fly, called *Cynips*, has the habit of laying its egg in such a wound. *Cynips* must have discovered that, once injured, the oak branch would always act in the same way, developing more and more cells in an attempt to heal itself. *Cynips* could do nothing but continue to injure oak twigs and lay its egg. The oak could do nothing but produce a perfect house, or incubator, for the egg for which the parent fly would take no more responsibility. The egg, once laid, develops into a wriggling, chewing fly larva. This, under the helpful protection of the gall with which the wounded tree surrounded it, changes into a fly—a full-grown *Cynips*, not unnaturally known as a gall fly. The matured fly eventually cuts its way out of the gall and disappears, leaving the gall to shrivel and dry.

Dr. McCook was a clergyman, and he well knew that, according to Biblical proverb, gall is bitter. He also was an entomologist and knew that ants usually had a taste for sweet rather than bitter. Yet here before him were ants busily lapping at tiny pearly-white spots which kept appearing on the surface of the galls in which *Cynips* larvae lay. The *Myrmecocystus* workers hurried from gall to gall as the pinpoints of white worked to the surface. The abdomens of some of the ants were already noticeably swollen with the result of their gathering.

Here, although McCook knew that he had in his grasp the answer to one more part of the mystery of the honey ant, was a problem which could not be solved in the field. With the help of his assistant, he cut off a gall-bearing branch without disturbing the ants working at it. Carrying it carefully back to the tent, he stuck it upright in a pail of water so that the ants could not escape and spent the rest of the night studying it.

The ants did not seem to realize that they were cut off from their nest, or else were so bemused by the entrancing substance which they were collecting that they did not care whether they were cut off or not. They kept on rushing from gall to gall, swallowing the dew drops which kept appearing.

Dr. McCook was able to determine by making several artificial nests and establishing colonies of *Myrmecocystus* in them, and by dissecting some of the oak galls, that the colony of ants used the exudation, or sweet sweat of the galls, as food. He was certain that the substance gathered was actually a liquid form of sugar. It has proved to be, in fact, chemically the same as grape sugar. The honey ant is a gatherer, not a manufacturer like the honey bee, since his sweet is already prepared for him by the interaction of gall-fly larvae and gall.

Why *Myrmecocystus horti-deorum* (ant of the Garden of the Gods), as the honey ant was afterward named, should use the bodies of his own kind as living barrels for the storage of the extra food which, like the honey bee, he only uses in case of famine or emergency, is still a mystery. The industrious ant must be not only industrious but patient and resigned. The repletes are willing to fill their crops, or let them be filled, with food of which they are passionately fond. The swollen crop pushes all the other organs of the abdomen flat against its tightly stretched walls. Once filled, these ants are willing to hang for the rest of their lives in the darkness of their miniature underground cavern, preserving their treasure for others who may never use it.

It is hard to imagine the state of consciousness of a worker *Myrmecocystus* coming home from the nocturnal harvest, having always been just a worker willing to gather honey and give it up to the stay-at-homes guarding the nest and tending the queen and her colony's young. Why some workers suddenly (or perhaps gradually) decide to give up the activities of the field and become—while most of their fellows go on as usual—jugs, vats, parts of a stockpile, is indeed a mystery. That, however, is just what a certain number of *Myrmecocystus* workers, not differing in bodily structure or social class or, so far as anyone knows, in intelligence, from their fellows do. What makes them do it? The repletes are not a separate caste. They are individual workers. Why does what motivates them not affect the others? Is it simply that each colony of honey ants requires just so many volunteers for the hanging-barrel corps, just so many and no more? Or, as with human beings, do some workers have an unusual taste for overeating and so condemn themselves to be reservoirs for others?

This is, perhaps, even beyond the discovery of the honey ant's identity and the source of his honey, the true mystery of *Myrmecocystus*. We do not know. We only know that every evening, when the sun sets over Pikes Peak and the hordes of honey ants go from the dark of their underground rock chambers to the dark of the shin oak copses, the decision is made for some of them, neither planned nor questioned, nor protested nor regretted. Every evening, too, while the active workers are out foraging, providing plenty of food for the colony, some of those hanging honey pots die unnoticed. Yet they continue to be groomed and tended, as if they were still alive, by those charged with such duty. Perhaps not for days does their death grip upon the ceiling relax. When it does, they fall to the floor. Only then are their attendants convinced that they are dead and must have their huge abdomens severed from their forward parts and both sections, the delicious liquor untasted, pushed and pulled through galleries and up corridors to the outer air and rolled without farewell into the colony's refuse pile.

3.

A Wolf in Search of a Name

When the first settlers from Europe came to New England 350 years ago, their chief problem was food. They found a heavily forested land full of wild animals and supposedly wild Indians. Both the animals and the Indians got their living from the land but their methods were not like anything known to the earliest English immigrants. Both wild creatures and wild men were, or were believed to be, hostile to the agricultural interests of the colonists.

The Europeans knew little or nothing about the land to which they had come. Yet they resolved to establish a means of subsistence similar to what they had known in the Old World. They did not know that European farming would work in America but they had to try it. They knew no other kind.

Little more of what is now New Hampshire than a strip of flat, somewhat rocky, but apparently fertile land along the seacoast was known to the European pioneers. Yet they did not hesitate to import cattle and begin dairy and beef farming. The first cattle were brought from Denmark to New Hampshire in 1631 by

Captain John Mason. It was not long before the settlers understood that the catamount—otherwise known as cougar, panther, puma, or mountain lion—and the wolf took kindly to this introduction of beef into their usual diet of venison and moose meat. The catamount, which required a great deal of territory to keep itself alive, could not survive in competition with human settlement as well as the wolf. For more than two hundred years the wolf was a dreaded enemy of man in northern New England. He outlasted, although not for lack of persecution, even the persecuted Indian.

The nineteenth century, as New England's population increased, saw a great change in the region's agriculture. Before 1800 Merino sheep could not be exported from Spain where the valuable breed was developed. In 1811, thanks to an enterprising New Englander, they were introduced into New England. For the next sixty years sheep determined the character of the countryside of Vermont, New Hampshire, and Maine. The forests were cut back to the very tops of the hills to make pastures for the increasing numbers of wool-bearing livestock.

This change in the environment meant that the wildlife of the area had to retreat northward. When the deer disappeared, the wolves which had preyed upon them as well as upon the settlers' cattle and sheep were seldom seen. Those which ventured to make forays into the open, hunting the hill country sheep, were shot or trapped for bounties of as much as ten dollars per wolf.

By 1870, when the western railroads had opened up vast areas for sheep raising, the production of wool in New England had begun to decline. For the next fifty years, the forest moved steadily back toward its original area, covering the less and less used hill pastures. The former sheep raisers moved down into the river valley towns. The deer returned, slowly, to the hills but the wolves apparently did not. They had become a legend rather than a fact. Between 1882 and 1895 bounties were paid on only twenty wolves. Although the bounty still was on the books in New Hampshire, nothing had been paid out since 1895. The wolf had become extinct, and everyone knew it.

Zoologists say that there were only two truly distinct wolf species in continental United States: the gray or timber wolf, and the Texas red wolf, which is sometimes black. The wolves which had lived in northern New England were gray or timber wolves—large creatures running up to one hundred pounds in weight. If they survived in the New England forest, it has been argued, hunters—who swarm through the woods like ants in the hunting season—would have been sure to have seen them at some time in the last seventy-five years. Even if the wolves themselves were not seen, it would have seemed likely that some of their kills, which seldom

were entirely eaten, would have been stumbled upon. The fact is that unless a wolf had been shot, photographed, or brought in for exhibition no one would have believed—and this is true of trained zoologists as well as unobservant sceptics among the lay citizens of the North Country—that what had been seen was anything but a wild dog. Since everyone knew that wolves did not exist in the northeastern forest, how could it be anything else but a dog?

Some seventy-five miles north of the Massachusetts border and perhaps 150 miles south of the Canadian line there is an area of nearly 25,000 acres which has been maintained as a game preserve for more than eighty years. It is surrounded by a well-maintained eight-foot fence, the existence of which, as a fence, the deer, elk, and wild boar that live in the preserve probably are unaware. It is quite a journey from one side of the area to the other and no animal can see both borders of the preserve at the same time. How, then, is a deer or boar to know whether he is on the outside or the inside of the fence? It is true that severe storms, particularly the hurricane of 1938, have sometimes leveled the barrier in places. Many of the preserve's animals have at such times found their way beyond the boundaries of the so-called park and become "naturalized" in the surrounding towns. Sometimes wild boar and elk have escaped in sufficient numbers to make things very difficult for farmers who were trying to grow corn. Yet these escapees were probably frightened by the storm in their home area and may have had a vague idea that, in crossing the broken-down fence, they were making their way into rather than out of some refuge.

It is true that some of the escapees from the preserve were not sponsored by natural causes but by natives of the surrounding region who, not liking the feudal aspect of a fenced-in 25,000 acres, cut holes in the barrier in what amounted to a kind of second-degree poaching. Perhaps the offenders regarded themselves as Robin Hoods, stealing from the rich for the benefit of the poor.

In the center of this preserve stands a mountain, just under three thousand feet high, whose rocky summit, crowned by a fire-lookout tower, rises above a series of waves of dense forest and open grassland. Much of this wild and beautiful area is very much like what the New England forest of 350 years ago must have been.

Within the bracken-carpeted shadows of this forest and across the open intervals range the wild creatures which are the special pride of those privileged to hunt within its borders.

The Virginia, or white-tailed, deer is by far the most abundant. The deer had always been supposed to have no real enemies other than the men who went into the park to shoot them. These hunters, if the truth be told, whatever their reasons for killing deer, did little more than keep the deer population down to a size which the preserve could support.

In the early spring of 1960 a number of things that happened in central New Hampshire directed attention to the game preserve and the region around it. Woodcutters who knew the forest well reported hearing strange wild howls which they had never heard before coming from the depths of the woods. It was even reported that one sturdy lumberman, well known as a hot-tempered fighter, working in the neighborhood, on hearing the strange, wild outcry picked up his equipment and went home. He could not face what he did not know. The noise seemed to him unearthly.

The staff of the game preserve began to find dead deer, ripped down their bellies and left uneaten. In a comparatively short time nearly fifty kills—certainly not made by man—were found inside and outside of the park. Most people, well aware that although a bounty on wolves was still on the books none had been paid for nearly seventy years, agreed that a pack of wild dogs must be responsible for the terror.

In April, 1960, the superintendent of the park, with a conservation officer and a skilled trapper, followed tracks in the snow leading up the great mountain which dominated the 25,000 fenced-in acres. The spoor led through dense thickets of spruce to a rock-fall near the base of the cliff forming the peak. Here the tracks of whatever creatures the men were seeking converged at what was plainly a den. Within this shelter were five tiny creatures which could not have been more than a day old each. No parents were to be seen. One of the party carried the five pups down the mountain in a sweater. They were turned over to Helenette and Walter Silver, biologists of the New Hampshire Fish and Game Department, to be raised and studied. As their small charges grew, the Silvers kept a complete written and photographic record of their growth and behavior.

While the Silvers were going about their study, outsiders continued to state their opinions as to what the animals were. Most uninformed people held to the wild dog theory. Some believed that the creatures were descendents of four wolves which had been imported into the park in 1907 by a local naturalist who intended to tame and train them. Two of these proved too hard to handle, however, and were disposed of almost immediately. A third died, and the fourth, a male, was kept for some time by the naturalist and exhibited at his lectures. This wolf died of a fit on Boston Common at the end of his master's leash. None of the four wolves were known to have had any young. Moreover, they were timber wolves and could hardly have produced in sixty-odd years a new and smaller variety such as the Silvers were studying. Many people who had heard of what was supposed to be a cross between a dog and a coyote and was referred to as a coy-dog believed the New Hampshire animals were just such a hybrid. The Silvers did not commit themselves publicly but they pointed out privately several things which seemed significant. For one thing, coyotes do not readily mate—especially in the wild—with other species, and the coy-dog, if it exists, is likely to be a man-made hybrid. Moreover, as later experiments showed, it is more likely to resemble a dog than a coyote. This the New Hampshire animals did not do. They resembled each other and they resembled wolves in coloration and marking. As they grew they became half again as heavy as a male coyote and 70 per cent heavier than a female coyote.

When they were old enough to mate, a male and a female of the captured litter were bred. They produced young which were all alike—resembling the first litter. On the other hand, members of the litters which were bred with dogs all came out looking and acting more like dogs than like wolves or coyotes.

It began to seem certain that while there was a possibility of hybridization long ago, the present animals were not hybrids. A hybrid is a creature which contains genes (which are the things which determine what an embryo animal is going to be) of two unlike characteristics. A hybrid will not breed true: that is, it will not, in mating, produce identical young. The New Hampshire animals did breed true and therefore had to be, not hybrids, but members of a definitely established species. Yet no one knew what the species was. The animals seemed like wolves but they also seemed like coyotes.

The New Hampshire Fish and Game Department sought the help of the Museum of Comparative Zoology at Harvard University and with the aid of a grant from the National Science

Foundation made a thorough study of the unknown animal.

While the study was going on, new specimens of the species kept turning up. In addition to the original five pups and fifty of their descendents, nearly sixty other specimens were taken in New Hampshire, Vermont, and Massachusetts between 1959 and 1966. Moreover, nearly fifty reported sightings of animals not killed were studied and verified.

The report of the scientists investigating the strange creatures was not completed and published until October, 1969. This report, prepared by Helenette and Walter Silver, makes it very plain that

there has for some time been in New England forests an animal without a name which is certainly entitled to one. The Silvers and Harvard University are of the opinion that the mysterious creature is a definite species evolved a considerable time ago from coyote and wolf. Possibly a trace of dog was involved, but long enough ago for the trace to have been bred out. After all, both wolf and coyote are dogs. The animal has now got a name: *Canis latrans, var.* (the "var." meaning "a variety of" or, in ordinary language, eastern coyote). The new mammal is nearer to the wolf in size than he is to the coyote, but there are many other characteristics which seem to make the name, coyote, suitable.

So far, so good. If our friend is a coyote, anyone killing him cannot collect the wolf bounty, a distinct advantage so far as the states in which he lives are concerned. Yet there is still a mystery. Where did the creature come from and how did he remain unknown for so long?

He is probably an immigrant, although many sightings during the last half century may have been ignored, since it was "known" that there were no wolves or coyotes in New England. It seems probable that the "new" eastern coyote came in from Canada, possibly by way of New York State. Most of the kills and sightings reported since the problem began to be studied have been made along, or close to, river valleys in New Hampshire and Vermont, a convenient means of access to the forests of northern New England.

New England's private wolf (the coyote is a form of wolf) has thus earned himself a name. Unfortunately, in doing so, he has become something real enough to shoot at. For this reason, in spite of his uncanny ability to conceal himself, he may not be with us very long.

4.

Who Killed Ectopistes?

WE OFTEN WONDER why scientists bother to think up elaborate names derived from Latin and Greek (and sometimes both) for creatures which everyone knows by some common name. There is a good reason. There can be only one scientific name and there could be, and often are, as many common names for a living wild thing as there are places in which it is found.

The fabulous passenger pigeon had many names from many localities. The native Indians of North America had at least twenty-one different words for the bird. In English there are close to a score of appellations given to it. The French, Dutch, and Germans knew it by as many more.

The passenger pigeon's one scientific name—the one which identifies it for all nations—is *Ectopistes migratorius.* This name, which the lost bird is stuck with, shows that even scientists with good ideas are not infallible. The two or three parts of an animal's scientific name are supposed to be descriptive of its structural characteristics—color, markings, habitat, what it eats, where it was first observed, or who first observed it.

In the case of the passenger pigeon there are only two names, one Greek and one Latin, each, rather foolishly, meaning the same thing. *Ectopistes* (and there is no other *ectopistes*) is from a Greek word meaning migratory, or often changing from place to place. *Migratorius*, from the Latin, means the same thing and therefore adds nothing to the first.

Curiously enough this double emphasis on migration in the name of the passenger pigeon has a rather tragic significance. It was, even more than was direct violence at the hands of man, the cause of the extinction of one of the most, if not *the* most, abundant vertebrate (animals with bony skeletons) ever to appear on earth. *Ectopistes*, the wanderer, when he met with adverse conditions, was unable to adjust his wandering to avoid them.

The early explorers of North America—that is, those who left written records—all indicate that along the entire Atlantic Coast from Virginia to Prince Edward Island the passenger pigeon existed in enormous flocks. Travelers, from Cartier (in 1542) on, reported great clouds of the birds, traveling day by day at high speed. Although it was impossible to count the thickness of the flying columns and the time it took them to pass, it was plain that the early pigeon population of North America must be reckoned in billions. Although the native Indians had always killed as many as they could for food and the early colonists did the same, there was no immediately noticeable diminution of their numbers. The pigeons fed upon what enabled both Indians and Europeans to survive—grain, berries, grapes, wild fruits, acorns, beechnuts, and chestnuts. Although both Indians and colonists found it easy to kill quantities of birds, the pigeons, at first, probably had the better of it, getting more of human provender than humans got in pigeon meat.

Ectopistes was a large and beautiful bird, the male being about seventeen inches long. Its coloring was blue and slaty gray on its back, the breast and throat were almost purple, and the back of the neck was iridescent in varying hues of bronze, green, and purple. It has been spoken of as one of nature's most magnificent creations. There can be little doubt that the awesome spectacle of millions of pigeons in flight, accompanied by the great noise of their wings, contributed to this appraisal. Yet nature seems to have applied grandeur to *Ectopistes* with a rather heavy hand.

The bird's food requirements were enormous—possibly as much as half a pint a day per bird. This, for the number of birds estimated by early travelers, would add up to nearly 18,000,000 bushels per day. When there was no serious competition and the great forest stretched unbroken from the Atlantic beyond the Mississippi, that amount of food in the form of acorns, chestnuts, beechnuts, rice, grapes, berries, tree seeds, and insects could be obtained without too much difficulty.

No one knows when the passenger pigeon first appeared in North America nor how long it took the species to build up to its maximum population, the number of which we can only guess. It may well have been between five and ten billion. Wild animals and birds of prey and a relatively thin population of Indians were *Ectopistes*' only apparent natural enemies. Yet there is considerable evidence that its numbers had begun to decline—at least in the northeast—before the white man came. It is a fact that within three hundred years of the first European settlements in North America, the last existing passenger pigeon died in the Cincinnati Zoological Park, in September, 1914.

This comparatively rapid extinction appears to point the finger of blame at civilized man. Yet there are many creatures, never in any age as abundant nor as strongly entrenched as *Ectopistes*, who have survived human depredation and still exist. Even the bison of the great plains outlasted, thanks to the efforts of the American Bison Society, man's savage and wasteful violence and has, though greatly diminshed in numbers, reached a point at which its population has to be controlled artificially. The Virginia deer, hunted and persecuted by Indian and white man alike, is probably more numerous today than it ever was. Coyotes have, as supposed enemies of the cattle and sheep ranchers, been slaughtered by the millions but they are still abundant.

It is perfectly true that man's attack upon *Ectopistes*, which reached its most savage height between 1860 and 1880, was the most thoroughly unscrupulous and violent campaign ever conducted against a wild animal, with the possible exception of the bison. Yet there is still some mystery in the utter completeness of the passenger pigeon's disappearance. The solution of the mystery must be looked for in the nature and habits of this remarkable bird. Suppose we regard all animal life as a great body of cells related to the world in which it lives. Then *Ectopistes* represents a kind of cancerous overgrowth of one type of cell—a growth not controlled by sound rule.

It is as if the passenger pigeon's life were like some machine invented by man which worked beautifully so long as gravity and friction were not involved. When conditions became such that gravity and friction could not be ignored, the machine failed to function. This was not wise nor far-sighted invention. There may be some reason why nature, in designing the passenger pigeon, was neither wise nor far-sighted.

There were many things about the life of *Ectopistes migratorius* which made things difficult for the bird. Most birds use several methods of maintaining a delicate balance between survival and the danger of overpopulation. Protective coloration, the building

of efficient nests in safe places, migration over great distances when the food supply is cut off by severe changes in weather, the ability or perhaps the instinct to lay a large clutch of eggs when there is great risk in raising a brood of young—these are all factors in bird survival.

The passenger pigeon availed itself of none of these. Its coloration offered no protection either in flight or at rest in the forest. Its nest was a flimsy structure hastily thrown together and crowded among dozens, even scores, in a single tree which often broke under their weight. *Ectopistes* laid a single egg (there were occasional reports of two, but one was the standard) and a strong wind could easily blow it from the thin platform of twigs which constituted the nest. In spite of its name, doubly suggesting migration, the pecularities of its wandering left it at the mercy of nature's irregular way of producing the food it required. Beechnuts, a favorite article of the bird's diet, were usually produced in any one locality only every second year. Chestnut and acorn crops were subject to weather conditions and could anywhere be a total failure. There no doubt were substitute crops, possibly in South America, which could have been used in emergency seasons. The passenger pigeons, however, never went to South America. The bird lived, either by compulsion or by instinctive choice, only in the eastern half of the United States and the southern one-fourth of Canada. Its range was roughly one-third of North America. It is possible that at its peak of population there were more passenger pigeons in that area than all other birds put together.

Something, some combination of circumstances, made the bird a great success if we count success merely in numbers, which we should not do, although we are inclined to think that man is a success because he has outnumbered all other vertebrates.

Ectopistes was not a success, however, in its ability to adapt itself to changing conditions. The noted ornithologist Ludlow Griscom said, "The primary cause for the passing of the passenger pigeon was its own specialized habits and a long list of biological 'defects.' Its low egg-laying capacity, flimsy nest, and herd instinct in migration are three minor ones. Its spectacular gregariousness was disastrous in two respects. The huge flocks could not be overlooked by the bird's enemies, and no effort was made to avoid them. In a primeval wilderness their ravages were overcome by the sheer weight of numbers. Every nesting involved an appalling mortality of adults and young and a waste of eggs caused by the habits of the bird itself. The final 'defect' of this pigeon was its inability to learn anything new; it could not change its habits to meet the pressure of new and unfavorable conditions or dangers."

When the forests fell before the advancing tide of human invasion, the bird could not alter its life-pattern and go where forests were yet untouched and food was to be had without troubling to look for it.

Ectopistes had to nest in the general area in which it had always nested. It had to seek food in places where food had always been found. Man learned that it was easy, as the tide of settlers moved westward, to find these places and to add to the pigeon's danger the cruel threat of wholesale trapping, shooting, and clubbing. This was the end. In spite of the efforts of some individuals and organizations who managed to get laws passed prohibiting the killing of pigeons on or near nesting grounds, the laws proved impossible to enforce. Unlike the bison, the pigeon was doomed.

Aldo Leopold, naturalist, conservationist, and author of *A Sand County Almanac*, said, "The pigeon was no mere bird, he was a biological storm. He was the lightning that played between two biotic poles of intolerable intensity: the fat of the land and his own zest for living. Yearly the feathered tempest roared up, down, and across the continent, sucking up the laden fruits of forests and prairie, burning them in a traveling blast. Like any other chain reaction, the pigeon could survive no diminution of his own furious intensity. Once the pigeoners had subtracted from his numbers, and once the settlers had chopped gaps in the continuity of his fuel, his flame guttered out with hardly a sputter or even a wisp of smoke."

When we think of the great waving flocks of birds darkening the sky for hours, even days, on end, seeming secure in their majesty of existence, we cannot help realizing that the mystery of "Who Killed *Ectopistes?*" has solved itself and left a greater mystery. Nature and the pigeon's disproportionate place in it were the cause of the bird's disappearance and man, whose place in nature seems also out of scale, had become the tyrant of nature.

The mystery is how did the flame of which Aldo Leopold speaks come to burn so brightly and for so long with such a wind of disadvantage blowing? And will man, whose flame has burned far more brightly, survive a threatened "diminution of his own furious intensity"? Can he say "no" to the passenger pigeon's history and continue to believe that nothing threatens him?

At least he can do something about the problem which *Ectopistes* could not do. He can think about it.

5.

The Generation Gap of the Lamprey

In a shallow pool formed by a ring of half a dozen rocks on the south shore of the St. Lawrence River between Cape Vincent and Clayton, the otherwise still water was lashed and churned by the spasms of a great fish dying. This was many years ago when one of the greatest of fresh-water fish, the sturgeon, was sometimes seen in the lower Great Lakes and the wide river which carries their waters northeastward to the sea. A small boy, on a beach picnic with his father and a boatman who knew the aquatic life of the St. Lawrence from many years of experience, stood and watched in terrified but delighted amazement as the sturgeon struggled to free himself from the circle of rocks and return to deep water. Something told the boy that this astonishing fish—at least six feet long, which is not large for a sturgeon—was doomed.

The excited boy called his father and the boatman, who identified the injured monster. The boy wanted to know why such a strong and sizable fish should find itself in such a desperate situation. Surely there could not be other, bigger fish in the river capable of giving a fatal wound to a six-foot sturgeon.

The boatman picked up a driftwood stick and pointed it at the sturgeon's side. Beneath a row of horny bosses, or plates, which extended from just behind the head to the beginning of the tail, were several red-raw circles with blobs of pinkish tissue streaming from them. The boatman, whose name was Ira, explained that these fearful wounds had been caused by something which he called a "lamper."

Ira, repeating folklore without knowing that that was what it was, told the boy and his father that the "lamper," or, more properly, lamprey, was a strange fish, like an eel in form and poisonous to human beings and other fish. It had, he said, in recent years found its way up the St. Lawrence from its home in the sea, into Lake Ontario and on through the Welland Canal around Niagara Falls to Lake Erie. It had managed this journey by clinging tc the bottoms of vessels bound upriver and through the Lakes. It had never found its way back, since it clings only to means of transportation which are going against the current.

The creature, according to Ira—whom the boy would have felt it a sacrilege to doubt—had some sort of sucking contrivance in its round mouth which not only enabled it to cling to the bottoms of moving ships but also to attach itself to other fish capable of giving it a ride. The fish on whose journeys the lamprey made itself a fellow passenger did not come off as well as the man-made vessels which also abetted its progress. For the lamprey was able to suck out the vitals of the fish to which it attached itself and leave the victim bloodless, with pale protruding entrails streaming from the gaping wounds on its side. Ira said that sturgeon, like the great lake trout and whitefish, had all but disappeared from the lower lakes as a result of the lamprey's taste for survival by parasitism.

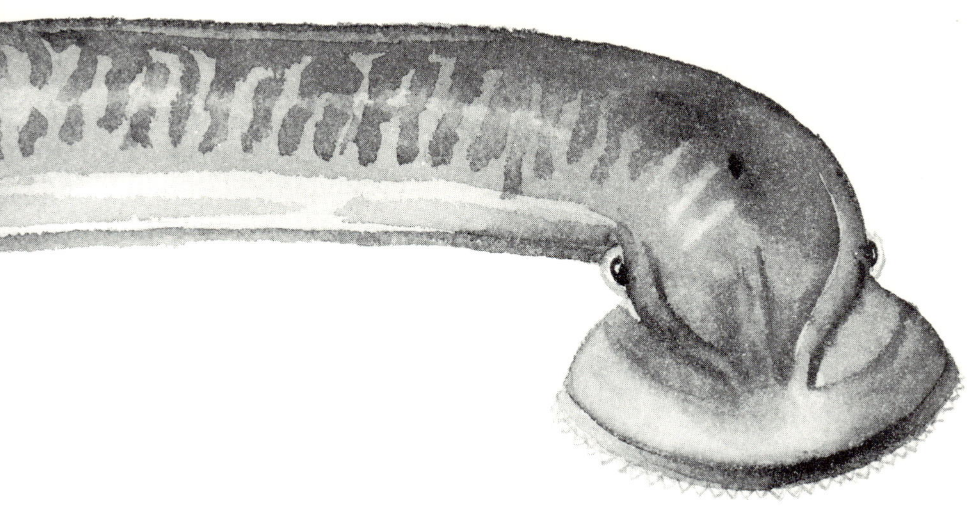

The boy was left with a confused feeling that the lamprey might be a superior being which had taken over the Great Lakes. The boatman declared that this apparently powerful creature seldom grew as much as two feet long but was, as the boy had seen, able to destroy fish three or four times its length and fifty or sixty times its weight. It was a long time before the boy had his first view of that unprepossessing creature, and even longer, in spite of asking and listening, before he learned anything significant and scientifically accurate about its incredible life history.

The boatman contended that lampreys were really dangerous to men, both because of their ability to cling to and bore into flesh and because of a poison in their teeth. The boy's father smiled, but he did not contradict Ira. Whether his father knew or did not know at the time, the boy learned much later that although a king of England was said to have died of eating lamprey, the flesh is not poisonous except during the last few days of the creature's life. At that time, because of the atrophy, or wasting away, of the alimentary canal and the consequent inability of bile and waste matter to find their way out of the lamprey's body, its flesh becomes green and unpalatable.

Ira said—and the boy believed it for a time—that for each year of a lamprey's life a new gill opening appeared on each of its sides, somewhat as a new rattle is added to the tail of a rattlesnake. It is true that the adult lamprey has seven gill openings on each side and that the probable life of the mysterious creature is something like seven years. The seven gill openings are, however, present, though at first not clearly marked, from the time the lamprey leaves its egg until it dies and are never more nor less in number.

It was something of a startling surprise for the boy to learn in later years that the unlovely lamprey, victor over his adored yet feared sturgeon, was not, as he had supposed, a superior being that had figured out ways of dominating his world. The lake lamprey is, in fact, not even a fish. It is a link between the primitive *Ascidians* (a low order of animal which includes the sea squirt), the *Amphioxus* (sometimes known as lancelet, which has no measureable heart or brain and colorless blood), and the true vertebrate fish.

How the lamprey got into the Great Lakes is not so much a mystery as a matter of dispute. It is said, in some authoritative works, that the lamprey only appeared in the Lakes after the opening of the Welland Canal that bypasses Niagara Falls. The Falls would have been too much even for such a resourceful traveler as the sea lamprey. Yet the differences in size and habits between the sea lamprey and the lake lamprey could not be accounted for if development of the lake lamprey took less than a hundred years. The Welland Canal was completed only in 1833. The lake lamprey was well established as a distinct variety before 1890. It seems much more likely that the lamprey species became landlocked long ago after the outlet of Lake Ontario had changed—because of upheaval and subsidence of the rocks at what is now the mouth of the St. Lawrence River. The waters of the Lake formerly made their way southward through the Mohawk and the Hudson Rivers.

The most fascinating part of the mystery of the lamprey was unsuspected for many years. In 1817 the French scientist, Baron Georges Cuvier, found an unknown, small water creature in the sandy silt of a creek bottom. He studied it carefully and finding in it, as he believed, no structural resemblance to any other form of life, gave it a name of its own. The strange thing was that it did have a shape, a structure, and a life of its own which to most scientists and all untrained people seemed entirely unlike anything known.

This tiny creature, to which Baron Cuvier gave the name *Ammocoetes* (from two Greek words, *ammo*, signifying sand, and *koete*, meaning bed), was blind and toothless, boneless, and translucent—that is, letting light through it. Its body, like that of a small, sharp-pointed pink worm, was segmented somewhat like that of a caterpillar. This tiny creature feeds itself by letting the silty water of the stream bottom enter its hooded mouth. By means of minute waving threads the little creature helps the organic matter in the water to sift through a tube in the back of its throat leading to the stomach and intestine. The constant passage of food though its body enables the *Ammocoetes* to grow slowly, without changing its bodily characteristics, for three or four years. During this time it gets along without eyes, without much of anything in the way of a brain and, for that matter, without even a true skull.

The real mystery of this primitive creature's life is in the unknown cause of a change which comes over it in the fall of its third or fourth year. Suddenly, in the course of a few weeks in winter, something happens to *Ammocoetes* which would have startled Baron Cuvier. The interior parts of its mouth begin an alteration which provides the tiny animal with a throat and teeth but no jaws. Eyes, which have been present but useless (being buried deep in the flesh), emerge and become usable. The long fin which ran from what would have been head, if it looked more like a head, to what would have been tail, if it had looked more like a tail, becomes two fins on the lower part of the back. The skull develops, in the form of cartilege rather than bone. The body loses its apparent division into segments and becomes smooth and slimy. The mouth is no longer a membranous sieve but becomes a purse-like circle lined with concentric rings of sharp, hornlike teeth. In

the circular center of the mouth appears a tongue, flattened at the end and equipped with several curved rows of teeth, a little finer than those of the mouth cavity. The seven rudimentary gill-openings of *Ammocoetes* become seven clearly defined holes. The little apparently aimless creature has become an adult lamprey, adult though primitive. He still does not have a real bone in his body and, henceforth, possesses an appetite no longer willing to accept only what the involuntary passage of water through him provides him with. The adult lamprey has an appetite for blood alone, the blood of fishes which it is now equipped to obtain and compelled to try to obtain. Yet, although it has now become a lamprey, it is still a lamprey-child, unable to mate and have offspring.

The adolescent lamprey's fish-blood diet, on which its sucking mouth and rotary drill teeth and tongue enable it to thrive, brings it to sexual maturity in something more than two years. When this culmination or climax of its doggedly ferocious adolescence is reached, the lamprey makes for some stream with a suitable bottom. Here both male and female work, as if they had been taught to do so, at the construction of a spawning ground.

A suitable bottom for the lamprey must satisfy many conditions. It must be a combination of fine sand and small stones in swiftly moving but not turbulent water. The mature lamprey's six or more years as an almost passive *Ammocoetes* and a bloodsucking, jawless creature, have not prepared him to consider the ultimate act of his life and decide what appurtenances will be required to ensure the performance of its function. He nevertheless goes about the preparation of his spawning ground as if he knew what he was doing. With the help of any females which happen to be about—and they are always there, each carrying with them from 25,000 to 40,000 eggs—he first builds a kind of barrage or weir of stones as large as jumbo hen's eggs. Then he cleans everything but sand from a space of two or three feet below the stones. At the lower end of this basin of sand he sets up another line of stones. It is worth noting that never before this time has it occurred to the mature lamprey that he could move stones, some of them exceeding his own body in weight. Yet he now does so, as if he had done it all his life, by placing his unpleasant sucking mouth against them, sucking hard and carrying the stone to the place to which his instinct has compelled him to assign it. This uncanny ability to work with stones has earned him his scientific name of *Petromyzon*, or "stone-sucker."

There is nothing haphazard or purposeless in *Petromyzon's* nest-building. The stones, arranged as they are when this curious—and doomed—creature has finished with them, cause enough variation in the flow of water over and between them to disturb the sand beyond and keep it in cloudy motion. We cannot solve the mystery of how the lamprey knows or, indeed, whether or not he does know, that this arrangement of the elements of his spawning ground is necessary. Yet it certainly seems to be.

When *Petromyzon* has completed his work and driven any extra males from the spot which he has chosen, he picks out a single female, seizes her by the back of the head with his sucking mouth, winds himself about her and holds her so tightly that it would be impossible for her not to discharge some of her eggs, which the male promptly fertilizes. During this process the eggs, some thirty or forty at a time, become mixed with the water-stirred sand which the writhing of the male lamprey's tail flails into still denser clouds. Since the eggs are sticky a certain number of them—by no means all—become attached to grains of sand and sink to the bottom, piling up against the downstream fence of stones. Crowds of greedy minnows hover about the spawning ground, darting in, when they get the chance, to gorge themselves upon stray eggs. The busy lampreys do not notice them. The male holds the female in his fierce and single-purposed embrace for as much as three or four days before all of her many thousands of eggs have been expelled. So tightly does he hold his mate that grains of sand lodging between them wear off parts of the skin where the bodies of the two creatures touch. When the spawning operation is finished and at least a considerable part of the eggs are safely buried in the bottom sand, the male and the female lamprey drift helplessly apart. Their bodily functions cease and they become a prey to fungus and disease. Neither male nor female will ever eat or mate again. Their emaciated, lifeless bodies drift downstream, their strange desperate work done—seven years of helplessness as *Ammocoetes* and of ferocity as adolescent lampreys exchanged for a few days of violent spawning and fertilization. Then, death and decay.

6.

Mystery: The Spider's Specialty

Spiders are so common and are found in so many places that the average person has a difficult time thinking of them as mysterious. To many they are unpleasant and often are regarded as bringing bad luck. French peasants have a saying to the effect that if you see—or perhaps it is kill—a spider in the morning, you will regret it all day long. Yet, the saying goes on, if you see or kill one at night, you will have even more reason to despair. It pays to look into sweeping statements like that. Those who have looked into the spider's ways have ended up with not only a sense of mystery but also a definite respect for the supposedly spooky creature.

The spider is not an insect but belongs to that very large group of living creatures (called a phylum) which includes crabs and lobsters, centipedes and millipedes, as well as insects, all with jointed legs. This phylum is called *Arthropoda*, which means jointed legs, six legs in the case of insects and eight in spiders. The million or more species of arthropods comprise three-fourths of all the known animals of the world.

The true mystery of the spider might easily be guessed from his name but for the fact that most of us become acquainted with him before we know the connection between his name and his activity. We would more readily do this if his name, spider, were not somewhat corrupted. It comes from the Anglo-Saxon verb *spinnan*, to spin, in the form of *spinthre* or *spinder*.

All spiders, like some insects (notably the silkworm), do spin in the sense that they are able to discharge a liquid through spinnerets in the lower part of the abdomen. This substance, once outside the body and drawn tight—perhaps with some assistance

from the drying effect of the air—becomes a solid thread of genuine silk. Spider silk, a complex fibre of what is called albuminoid protein (sometimes referred to as scleroprotein, *sclero* meaning hard or insoluble), is a remarkable product for a completely instinctive creature like a spider to have developed. It is, in fact, one of the most remarkable of animal products and the spider's life is completely dependent upon it.

There surely can be no one who, whether curious and interested or not, has not seen a spider's web and does not realize that it is an ingenious device for trapping its maker's necessary food. Spider silk, however, is used for more than snares. There are very few spiders that go anywhere without pulling along behind them a sometimes invisible line of silk, known as a dragline, by means of which they are able to return to their base without bothering to remember where it is. As the spider has an almost infinitesimal and very limited brain, this is probably just as well.

Spider silk, once it leaves the spider, cannot be returned into the creature's body. It is therefore not strange that it should be so common in places which are not regularly cleaned, such as attics and cellars. It would not necessarily be expected, however, that spider silk would be so abundant in the open air that in certain parts of the world at certain times of the year it may descend in sheets and streamers from the night air and be found in the morning lying like a veil of silver over the countryside. This it does do, and what falls and becomes silvered by the dew was long ago given a name which, no doubt after many changes, has become the word *gossamer.* (This name is also applied to any very fine gauzelike fabric.) Gossamer is accounted for in several different ways, depending on the person providing the explanation. Most explanations of how gossamer got to be called gossamer are quite primitive and do not associate the dew-pearled sheets of silver with such a despised source as the spider. In Christian countries such as Germany and France the phenomenon was thought to be a kind of symbolic annual representation of the aftermath of the assumption into Heaven of the Virgin Mary, the filmy threads of gossamer being the fibres of Mary's winding sheet abraded and torn from her as she was transported through the skies toward her celestial home. In parts of France these delicate fibres were known as *gaze à Marie*, which can be converted without great trouble to gossamer. The more likely explanation of the word is in its relation to the season of the year which we know as "Indian summer" but which in northern Europe is, or was, sometimes referred to as "goose summer," the time of year when geese begin to migrate. This is the time when true gossamer is found in the greatest abundance—particularly in northern Europe, England, Scotland, and northeastern United States.

Whatever our primitive ancestors may have thought of the origin of this exquisite substance, they did not have sufficient knowledge of the animal world to associate it with the furtive creature which has always seemed so repulsive to most people. In fact, in the sixteenth century the poet Edmund Spenser referred to gossamer as if it were dew scorched by the sun, and in the mid-nineteenth century James Thomson, who as a naturalist should have known better, did the same thing.

Today, the marvels of the world of spiders are waiting to be discovered and explained in every library. Yet comparatively few people, young or old, are aware of the fact that these creatures, like men, were born earth-bound but have—in ways that are not so different, although they are called instinctive rather than intelligent—learned to extend their range by travel in water and through the air.

In both these elements the spider's success has been achieved with the help of its remarkable ability, unmatched by anything in the bodily function of man, to produce silk thread. This thread, or silk, is elastic—capable of being stretched by 20 per cent of its length. It is waterproof, and of a tensile strength considerably greater than steel wire of equal size.

A spider known as *Argyroneta*, the water spider, which is found in Europe and parts of Asia, has, without any apparent reason for departing from the ways of other spiders, taken up life in the water.

Argyroneta, whose name means "silver-spinner," is not very different from any half-inch long, plain, dark-brown spider. She has no special organs or members to enable her to live under water or to swim. She has to breathe air like other spiders and yet she does live under water and she does swim, if not exactly "like a fish" at least as successfully.

Argyroneta—or, rather, let us call her the water spider since she is the only known spider living entirely under water—in spring, after a winter hibernation deep in some pond or stream, builds a platform of silk beneath the surface. This is suspended from, or rather tightly fastened to, the stems of a group of underwater plants. This flexible layer of webbing is very closely woven and, from the surface of the water, almost invisible. When it is completed the water spider swims to the top of the pond or stream, lifts her abdomen and hind legs above the water and quickly lowers them again. She has entrapped a large bubble of air, which her extended hind legs with their wavy hairs keep from escaping as she swims down to her prepared dwelling place. Once under the platform she releases the bubble of air, which rises under the mat of silk and cannot escape back to the surface of the pond. *Argyroneta* repeats this process many times until the silken sheet of the platform is transformed into a bottomless dome of air, its own pressure keeping the water out as the pressure of air in a human diving bell does. This supply of air is maintained in careful balance by the spider. When there is too much air the creature cuts a hole in the tiny dome and lets some out, sealing the hole up again at the proper moment. When there is too little air, it being consumed too rapidly by the active spider's demand for oxygen, she swims gracefully to the surface and brings down enough bubbles to replenish the supply. No one knows exactly how she knows when the air pressure in her underwater tent is too great or too little.

At night, *Argyroneta* spends most of her time hunting—always under water—for small water creatures which she drags to her diving bell to chew and digest. The male of the water spider is—fortunately for him, and unlike many other spiders—larger than the female. She might resent his drain upon her oxygen supply when he moves in, or, as he sometimes does, builds a slightly smaller dome nearby which he connects with the female's by a silken tunnel.

After mating, when the eggs are laid, they are suspended in a small bag of toughly woven silk from the top of the silvery water palace. When, after about three weeks, several hundred small spiders hatch, they move down and crawl about among their mother's eight legs and over her back until something tells them

it is time to go out on their own. They do not have to learn to swim, although they have nothing more with which to swim than any other dry-land spider has, nor any better brain with which to master the art of moving about under water. The young water spiders do not try to rise to the surface and take a chance on adventure in the mysterious world of the land. They do, unquestioningly, what their parents have done. They are, and they remain, water spiders. Without ever having seen their parents prepare for winter, they follow the same pattern of behavior, building a small closed sac under water, in some snail shell or cavity in rock or wood. To this they retire, looking like a drop of quicksilver, with a bubble of air large enough to supply their need for oxygen in a dormant state for three or four months.

The water spider, as has been said, is not found throughout the world. There is one fairly obvious reason for this: her manner of living does not allow for distant travel and also makes it unlikely that her eggs or young will be picked up by birds or other insects and carried to distant lands.

There are, however, other spiders, perhaps the majority of members of the class *Arachnida* (which is the spiders' section of the *Arthropoda*), who have equally remarkable habits. Spiders, although wingless, mastered millions of years ago the art of heavier-than-air flight which has proved so troublesome to man. Here again, it is that mysterious substance, spider silk, which has provided the means, as it has provided the means by which *Argyroneta* is able to live under water.

Earlier it was mentioned that sheets and strands of gossamer were found at certain times in certain places, notably England, northern Europe, and northern North America. This occurrence of quantities of the gathered fibres of spider silk, although mysterious enough to have kept simple country people guessing for centuries, is not accidental.

Men have known for a long time that spiders are often found in places which, according to reason, they could not possibly have reached. Charles Darwin, in the course of his great voyage on board the *Beagle*, recorded that on November 1, 1832, while the ship was some sixty miles from shore in the mouth of the Rio de la Plata, he noticed that the rigging was coated with films of web of what he called the "Gossamer Spider." The weather was fine and clear and the air was "full of patches of the flocculent web as an autumnal day in England." Darwin noticed that the stays, sheets, and sails were covered by some thousand small, dusky red spiders, not more than a tenth of an inch in length, each attached to a single thread of web rather than to the patches of gossamer. Dr. Henry McCook, author of the great work in its field, *American Spiders and Their Spinning Work*, says that while he was crossing the Atlantic in the winter of 1881-82 on the American liner *Pennsylvania*, the ship's captain, George H. Dodge, told him a similar story. While his vessel was sailing along the eastern coast of South America in March (1881) at a distance of two hundred miles from shore, the ship was covered with spider webs containing spiders. "The spiders," said Captain Dodge, "seemed like elongated balls with a sort of umbrella canopy above them. They settled upon the sails [in the 1880's sails were still used in combination with steam] and rigging and finally disappeared as they came."

For a long time it was supposed that there was a particular form of spider which had developed skill as an aeronaut. Few could believe that any creature so earth-bound as the average spider could possibly take to the air. Yet careful study has shown that almost all varieties of spider, with the probable exception of some of the great primitive types known as *mygalomorpha* (of which the tarantula of the western hemisphere is one) and, of course, *Argyroneta*, the water spider, can and do fly as man has learned to fly. Spider flights take place during all of the warm weather months but chiefly in spring and fall.

The orb weavers, which include the beautiful black and orange garden spider, *Argiope*, are so devoted to their spectacular circular, geometrically designed web that they are almost helpless away from it. They are, nevertheless, at a certain point in their lives, mysteriously compelled to leave the earth entirely, if temporarily.

Argiope lays, on an average, something like a thousand eggs—while she is hanging upside down from her web, laying the eggs upward upon a previously prepared skin of tough silk. Over this skin she places a kind of spider-eiderdown of a consistency entirely different from that of the basic skin. Above this layer of down she spins a covering of brownish silk. On this she deposits her eggs, prefertilized but coated with a sticky substance containing additional sperm which she has kept stored within her body. Once the eggs are laid and cemented in place, another layer of white or yellowish silk is spun over them. Over that comes still another layer of yellowish-brown, fluffy down and, finally, an extra covering of closely spun tawny fibre which soon hardens into something like parchment paper. This pear-shaped mass protects the eggs from predators, insect or other, and from the weather as well.

The development of young spiders in their eggs within this safe and comfortable sac is quite unlike the development of the young within a bird's egg. In the first place the mother spider does not brood her eggs, although while she lives she does keep enemies away from the sac. In many cases the female spider, whose life span is not much more than a year, does not live to see her young emerge from their cocoon. In the second place, when the individual egg hatches within the sac, it is not a finished spider which emerges but a curious creature, swathed in membranes, which can neither feed nor spin but which is nourished by a mass of egg yolk in its abdomen. After a short period of growth it becomes necessary for this creature to molt, or shed its skin, in order to move into the next larger size. This is the beginning of the spider as it will be. It is still, however, enclosed with its hundreds of sisters and brothers in the cover sac. What happens next is dependent upon the weather. If it is cold, nothing happens—perhaps for a whole winter. If it is warm the young spiders band together and either cut a neat hole in the sac or rip its sides if the material is weak enough.

When the tiny spiders emerge, like a small army, from their comfortable but crowded nursery, each is on his own. There is usually no mother to guide or encourage them.

Instead of dispersing downward through twigs and stems of grasses toward the earth where they will eventually live out their lives, the young spiders begin ascending whatever object of any height is near at hand. They keep spinning all the time and leaving draglines behind or attaching silk to nearby projections of grass or bush. These random lines of silk are constantly being broken and blown away, forming bundles of gossamer, but the little spiders keep on going higher.

One group may climb a fence post and stand together on its flat top. One by one, each spider faces into the wind, raises its abdomen, or rear end, extends its hind legs upward and from its spinnerets produces a series of short silken threads. These are

caught and drawn out by whatever wind is blowing. When a spider feels a sufficient tugging from the wind it lets go of the fence post to which it has been holding with its forelegs and is carried off into the air—upward if the air currents are blowing in that direction or parallel with the ground if the wind is strong. The spider can manipulate his flight to a certain extent by climbing up the blowing threads which have issued from its spinnerets and are kept streaming upward by the air currents. If the filaments are too long the spiders roll them up (they cannot pull the silk back into their bodies). If they are too short, the aeronauts sometimes weave silk about their legs to make baskets of their bodies, held up, instead of by a gas bag, by the incredibly light, waving strands of fibre blowing in the air above them.

No one knows exactly how far a spider may travel in a single flight, but his ability to fly is, for the brief season during which he is compelled to indulge it, almost unlimited. No matter when he comes down, he is always able to climb another weed or post to fly again. Yet this miraculously acquired ability to make use of spider silk to extend the range of the creature who produces it is not, as we have seen, the main benefit which its skill as a spinner provides. Moreover, the spider is, and remains, a groundling with only a seasonal or, perhaps, wayward interest in travel by air. Many spiders that can and do fly have not noticeably extended their range by aerial dispersal, and it is not only the pressure of newborn population on the young which induces them to travel by air since adult spiders often indulge themselves in the luxury.

Scientists, looking for traces of life in the upper air, have found spiders ballooning comfortably at ten thousand feet, not, it is certain, of their own volition. The notion of flight, however, entertained for so brief a part of their lives and then forgotten, is what put them at the mercy of the winds and updraughts of the air.

It is probable that we shall have to admit that the spider itself is the mystery.

7.

The Safety of Danger

It is sometimes difficult for the ordinary, nonscientific person whose acquaintance with ants comes only from those adventurers who reach kitchen sugar boxes and syrup bottles to understand the extraordinary complexity of ant society. Those who know the mysteries of ant life realize that there are few more interesting creatures.

Men have, for thousands of years, noticed the industry and apparent intelligence of ants. Moralists have used these qualities to reproach human beings for their failure to solve their life problems as ants do.

"Go to the ant, thou sluggard; consider her ways, and be wise," says the Bible (Proverbs 6: 6). In the seventeenth century the Cavalier poet, Richard Lovelace, referred to the same creature as "thou great, good husband, little ant." Of course, Lovelace was using the word "husband" in its now almost lost sense, to mean a cultivator, tiller of the soil, provider of food. As a "husband" in today's common usage of the word, the ant has more than one problem. In the first place, most ants are females and there is considerable evidence that to the greater part of the ant colony husbands, as such, are not at all necessary. The reasons for this sexual independence are extremely complicated and the scientists who study insects (entomologists) are not entirely in agreement about them even today.

Ants are, without doubt, the most numerous of living creatures. They are found in unbelievable numbers everywhere in the world except in the seas and on the Antarctic continent. They are completely social animals—that is, they cannot pretend to survive without the cooperation of their fellows. In this, ants are like men, although human beings do not always admit such dependence upon others.

Ant societies, of which there are many types, were developed to their present state as much as a million years ago, long before man had emerged from the apparent darkness of his primitive past. Consequently, since ants identical in shape and behavior with those of the distant past are still alive, it can be said that their social organization as well as their physical structure has been successful. There have been some narrow escapes, however, one of which is the main subject of this discussion.

Man has not lived long enough for it to be said of him that his society and his physical equipment are as successful as the ant's. Indeed, we do not need to look farther than the newspapers and television to find suggestions to the effect that the organization of man's society is far from perfect. Like the ant's, human society has had many narrow escapes, but unhappily for man, he is still in danger.

Our literature provides nothing but praise for the ant, though as a living creature he is not quite as perfect as he is made to appear. The tendency of ants to lavish extravagant care upon their offspring, to spend their time working themselves to death, to serve their queens with unquestioning loyalty, may not be what those tendencies appear to be.

An animal society is a group which is organized for the purpose of making use of the special skills and equipment of its members to further the interests of the group as a whole. We know that in human society this purpose is often lost sight of by individuals. So far as we are able to discover, ants have no way of having individual opinions. The interests of an ant society are focused on the birth, care, and development of the young and the gathering and storage of food.

In human society there are only two definite types of individual —physical types, that is: male and female. In ant societies there are many different physical types. Each may be different from the others in both form and function. Among ants the workers—which may be found in large, medium, or small sizes—are always females. Workers in human society are, of course, both male and female and their work does not always appear to be concerned with the care of the young or with the gathering and safekeeping of food. Neither males nor females, among humans, are kept from having children by the fact of being workers. It is, however, true that both sexes are often kept by their employment from taking proper care of their young.

Among the ants, taking proper care of the young is the main

task of the workers. In fact, the worker ant is so specialized as nurse, babysitter, guardian, and housekeeper that her attention to the young sometimes seem to human beings to be abnormal. It is probable that some peculiarity of the young, such as the exudation of a sweet discharge, gives the workers' charges a flavor which the adults cannot resist and which induces the caretakers to keep licking and scraping at the young. Perhaps it is this, rather than instinctive devotion, which has led us to suppose that ants are more diligent in caring for their progeny than humans are.

Whether or not there is any basis for this suspicion that the ants' treatment of their young is not entirely altruistic, the behavior of these tiny creatures toward their eggs and larvae has some risks attached to it. There are creatures other than humans who have noted the apparently fierce devotion of worker ants to their young. It has occurred to many such creatures—for the most part, small beetles—that such reasonless single-mindedness might be made use of. Many insects, from mites to beetles, have in some way discovered that it is possible to live in an ant colony without being noticed—certainly without being persecuted—and to get for themselves and their own young a share of the care and nourishment which their involuntary hosts believe that they are providing for ants only.

These invaders, although not all of them show any more genuine devotion to the ants than the ants do to their own younger set, are know as myrmecophiles, or ant lovers. Some of them merely live unnoticed in the tunnels of their hosts, surviving on particles of liquid nourishment dropped by the ants. Others take a more positive view of their social parasitism, learn the habits of the creatures with whom they live, and snatch droplets of food as they are passed from ant to ant in the dark passages of the ant colony. Still others have habits which are a distinct threat to the very structure of ant society.

These parasites upon the social life of the ant are attracted by the ant's tendency to accept anything moving within the chambers and passages of its colony as one of its own. Some of the intruders, however, carry their parasitism much farther than merely living in ant hills or subterranean cities as passive or unnoticed guests. They seem to realize, as has been suggested, that the ants' passion for licking, scraping, and polishing their eggs and larvae is the result of a taste for sweet substances secreted by the young. Many species of small beetles have developed an ability, like that of the ant children, to exude vapors and liquids which the ants, once having tasted, cannot do without. These clever parasites become more than merely tolerated guests. Dangerous though they may be, they become a necessity to the ant.

A group of European beetles known as *Lomechusini* have carried ant parasitism to a point at which, were certain mysterious balances not in operation, it could easily destroy the society and colony of the addicted ant.

To explain why this is true, it is necessary first to explain that an ant colony is, in some ways, like the colony of living cells which compose the human body. If the cells are permitted to develop and function normally, the colony, or body, will be healthy and survive. If anything disturbs the development of the cells, or

speeds them up abnormally as cancer does in the human body, the body or colony will be thrown out of balance and will produce deformities or abnormalities which may lead to death.

If something disturbs the cells of which the body is composed—a cut or a wound, for instance—they set to defending themselves against the injury caused. The wound will either heal, or infection might set in.

Similarly, if you were to thrust a broad-bladed knife into the side of an ant hill you would see the ants, which are the compound cells of the ant colony, rush about in an equal effort to heal the wound in the body of the colony. Neither the cells of a human body nor the ants of an ant society can act as individuals. Their response to any external or internal threat to the mass of which they are the living grains must be for the benefit of the society of organisms which encompasses and includes them.

The chief difference between a human and an ant society is the result of man's mysterious ability to think in terms of cause and effect. Man is, in fact, able to alter the face and course of his social life by making use of both memory and foresight. The ant, which has been able to develop many remarkably durable forms of society, can only use the limited brain which he has been given. He cannot pass laws saying that, for the sake of society, he must do this and must not do that.

Most true insects go through a development involving several stages. First the egg, then the larva—a kind of active embryo—then the pupa, a stage in which the larva rests and changes into a mature insect and, lastly, the imago, or finished creature.

The mystery of ant survival is illustrated by the case of an ant known as *Formica sanguinea,* the blood-red slavemaker, whose taste for the golden hairs on the flexible abdomen of the beetle *Lomechusa strumosa* bears some unpleasant resemblance to man's

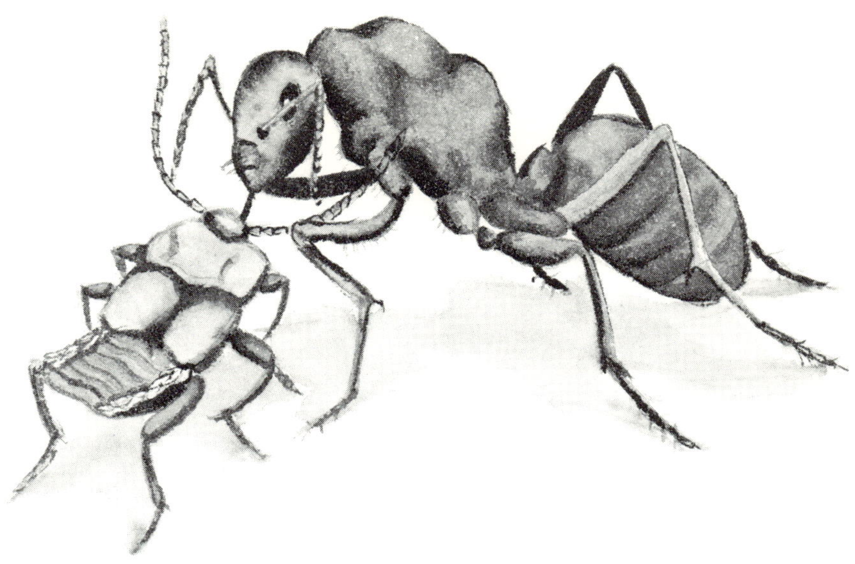

taste for alcohol and drugs.

Lomechusa's young, which of course have to be brought up in the ant colony since the beetle never leaves it, are quiet creatures who are far more sinister than their passivity suggests. They tickle the ants with their antennae, or "feelers," and get fed drops of honeydew in response to their tickling. The ants, captivated by the adult *Lomechusa's* fascinating golden hairs with their intoxicating nectar, do not mind the insistence of the *Lomechusa* larvae. They are apparently quite unaware that these same larvae lie quietly among their own young, chewing them to bits. The ants even seem to feel, for some reason, that the *Lomechusa* larvae are more worthy of attention than their own, as if they were simply a better grade of ant larvae. This feeling induces them to take scrupulous care of the young beetles and to neglect their ant children.

The flourishing *Lomechusa* devour the larvae of *Formica sanguinea* and reduce their numbers, causing a lack of balance in the ant brood. The *sanguinea* queen larvae, as a result, develop abnormally, either because they are neglected or because the *sanguinea* nurses try to convert them into workers to replace the losses of that caste resulting from the appetites of the *Lomechusa* young. These abnormal queens become lazy and incompetent, and are really neither workers nor queens. They have the effect of diseased cells on the ant colony. The mystery is here. Why does not the spread of the disease brought on by the ants' passion for what *Lomechusa* has to offer result in the ultimate death of the ant colony?

The answer is that, as has been suggested, the *sanguinea* workers do treat the *Lomechusa* larvae like their own in one all-important sense. *Formica sanguinea* always covers its grown larvae with soil so that they may spin their cocoons and become pupae, which is the next stage before the mature insect. When the cocoons are finished, the worker ants dig them up, clean and pile them in nursery chambers.

It just happens that the larvae of the parasite beetle, *Lomechusa*, also have to be covered with earth in order to become pupae. Here is the answer to the mystery. The *Lomechusa* larvae, which, unlike those of the ants, do not spin cocoons, have to be left buried in order to develop. Since the ant workers apparently do not know the rules of *Lomechusa* development, they treat all the young in the colony alike, digging up the *Lomechusa* pupae as well as their own. The unearthed *Lomechusa* cannot survive this treatment. It is only because the ants do not happen to locate all the *Lomechusa* pupae that the race of beetles survives, in numbers sufficient to begin the confusing life cycle all over again but not in sufficient numbers to destroy the ant colony.

It is somewhat terrifying to realize how chance and accident must often be depended on to preserve the balance between life and death. Men should be in less danger from their habits than ants and beetles, because they are able to think about cause and effect and so depend less on chance.

8.

Bird of Paradox

ALTHOUGH MOST PEOPLE are inclined to lump all penguins together and think of them as clowns of the zoo, there are vast differences among them. The Emperor, the most striking and largest variety in the family, is the least known. The living mystery of his existence is either not known at all or so misunderstood that it might as well be forgotten.

To begin with, the Emperor penguin is a bird, but it is as incapable of locomotion in the air as man was before balloons or airplanes were thought of. He can move freely only in water. He is a bird, but unlike most birds, he chooses for his breeding grounds not a latitude teeming with insects and grain, with trees to nest in, but instead the most inhospitable land in the world, the Antarctic continent. Moreover, his perversity is such that, as if to say that we have seen nothing yet, he chooses not the comparative mildness of Antarctic summer but the very depth of winter, the season of 100-mile-an-hour winds, blizzard snows, and temperature of from 40 to 70 degrees below zero, in which to incubate his eggs.

As if further to demonstrate his determination to shame other birds, he chooses, too, to build no nest. Perhaps it is putting it strongly to say that he chooses, for, in fact, he has no choice since his rookeries provide no nesting materials, not even loose pebbles such as are available to his less austere cousins, the Adélie penguins. His substitute for a nest is a kind of balancing act. Between two feet shod like a circus clown's, upon which he waddles somewhat as Charlie Chaplin used to do, he balances a single egg where, if he were a man, the tongues and laces of his shoes would be. This feat is accomplished with the aid of a feathered flap of skin depending from his lower belly and fitting the egg like a parka. In this extraordinary position—looking somewhat like a man without a belt whose trousers have slipped to his feet—the male Emperor carries the egg for two whole months, while the female, who merely laid the egg and passed it in his direction, heads for an eight-week round of heavy eating miles away at the edge of the Antarctic ice.

Apparently perfectly satisfied with this arrangement, the male bird gathers with a crowd of equally equipped fathers and stands in the darkness waiting. When the terrifying Antarctic hurricanes blow across the rookery and the sandy snow rides the wind like a gathering of shotgun pellets crossing the sound barrier, all the Emperor can do is huddle a little closer to his fellows and turn his back to the storm. When the wind abates he is able to move around a little, but there is not much point in his moving, for he can see practically nothing since the period of incubation corresponds with the darkest period of polar night.

There is little for him to do. True, when there is twilight or dawn light, he and his fellow Emperors indulge in a little sporting ceremony known to ornithologists as "display." During incubation, or immediately after hatching, these weird birds often gather in a group about one of their kind and, with a mandarinlike bowing of their necks, stare at him. What the Emperors stare at is the flap of skin between the subject's legs, which he lifts obligingly, exhibiting an egg or a chick, according to the point in incubation at which the display takes place. During this ceremony the bird indulges in what could be called crowing, though the sound—almost musical and quite different from the standard Emperor voice which is not unlike the sound of the horn of a diesel locomotive—does not even remotely resemble the crowing of a cock.

If there is little for an incubating penguin to do, there is even less for him to eat. The sea is frozen for miles from where he stands and even where the wind exposes black and jagged rocks nothing, usually not even lichen, grows upon them. The normal food of the bird consists of crustaceans such as crabs and cephalopods, largely repesented by the smaller squids. In the stomach of one moderate-sized penguin dissected by scientists were found the parrotlike beaks and part of the bodies of twenty good-sized squids, each when alive having been about a foot long, not counting tentacles. If you were used to having this sort of thing in your

stomach, it would be quite a trial to have nothing whatever there for two months.

The Emperor's method of propagating his kind seems, to say the least, impractical. It is very different from the comfortable incubation of birds in tropical and temperate regions where the brooding parent may at least sit on a well-arranged clutch of eggs and be fed by her own industry or by a careful and busy mate.

Birds in any climate are busy after their young are hatched, providing in food for their brood from 40 to 60 per cent of the weight of each young one daily. It would not be strange if they sometimes were exasperated by the cavernous upstretched maws beneath them and wished that they were in the Antarctic. They do not know how well off they are!

When the Emperor penguin's chick emerges from the shell, there is no one but a leg-weary father who has been standing erect for two solid months to welcome it to the world—leg-weary and himself hungry, since he has not had so much as a snack in all that time.

It might be supposed that this uncomfortable way of arranging its domestic life would be the death of the Emperor penguin tribe. Here is where the mystery lies. This amazing creature is not just a perverse rebel determined to do things the hard way. Actually his very insistence on doing things which other birds would not do is what keeps him alive today.

When we think of man's struggle for physical existence and his, so far, amazing success at it, we are inclined to ascribe it to his superior mental qualities. The Emperor penguin has no superior mental qualities—in fact, few mental qualities of any kind other than those which intensify his skill in using his physical equipment. If instinct were not such a controversial word, it would be suitable

to say that the Emperor is simply a bundle of instincts which so fill his life that he has little need of reasoning power.

It is not reasoning power which has made him turn in a direction opposite to other penquins and take up a residence farther south, there adapting himself to conditions which we who observe him believe, whatever the facts may be, that he need not endure. Whatever caused the Emperor penguin to turn south instead of north has not betrayed him into extinction. He has, as will be seen, made, for no apparent reason, one of the most extraordinary adaptations to environment made by any living creature.

The Emperor is a bird, but he does not fly, he does not build a nest, he does not make melodious sounds. The only thing which he has in common with all birds is feathers.

Before going on to explain the logic of this strange bird's contrariness, it might be well to have a look at him. Unlike some of his smaller relatives, he does not thrive in captivity. Those who have seen penguins in zoological parks have usually seen the Adélie or the Galapagos penguin, both very much smaller. The Emperor is one of the bulkiest of birds, weighing sometimes more than ninety pounds and averaging, for an adult, as much as seventy. A full grown one may have a chest measure of from forty to fifty inches.

Emperors are, it should be said, quite beautiful birds. Dr. E. A. Wilson, the first man to make a careful study of them, said ". . . their lemon yellow breasts shone like satin in the sun, and their bluish backs and jet black heads set off the golden yellow patch on the side of the neck, and the rose or lilac streak on the lower bill. The back and breast, if the bird had just been in the water, would glitter with crystals of ice and salt."

All this for an eyeless, breathless, heartless world!

Like all the penguin tribe, the Emperors travel, when on land, either in a humanly erect position or in a posture which used to be known in sledding parlance as "bellywhoppers." In this latter fashion, propelling themselves by vigorous strokes of their flippers, they can manage speeds up to ten miles an hour.

They have prodigious strength, being able to break a dog's leg with a stroke of a flipper or to inflict a painful and lasting bruise on a man. Once some whalers who tried to capture one fastened belts about his body in order to keep the bird from delivering right and left hooks with his flippers while being transported. The Emperor simply took a deep breath and the belts snapped like paper!

In spite of this extraordinary strength, the Emperor is not belligerant. Many birds have a strong sense of what is called "territory." The male of a pair will stake out a claim, usually in the vicinity of the nest, and defend it against all comers of his own kind. This sense of territory makes birds bellicose and irritable. Not so with the Paul Bunyan of birds, the Emperor penguin. He has no nest, there is no food to be kept from others, and territory means nothing to him. Strong as he is, he doesn't fight, except to defend himself, a kind of fighting at which he gets little practice since, when he is on land, he has no enemy but man (although the skua, a fierce Antarctic bird, attacks young penguins in the spring). The Emperor even rests his head and flippers on the shoulders of his own kind when they huddle together in a storm while he is incubating, something which other birds would never dream of doing.

This mighty fowl has been known to man for perhaps a century and a half. Indeed, as Dr. Robert Cushman Murphy has suggested, it was the Emperor penguin that first gave scientists the idea that there were continental lands at or about the South Pole. An Emperor taken in 1841 by the United States Exploring Expedition between what has been called Wilkes Land and the Balleny Islands was found to have basaltic pebbles in his stomach. The presence of these was taken to indicate land, as yet undiscovered, to the south.

It was not until the British National Antarctic Expedition of 1901-04 that any extensive study of the Emperor was made. Yet, as the rookeries where its young are born are few in number and relatively inaccessible, little or nothing was even then learned of the bird's extraordinary breeding habits. The Emperor was indeed a mystery. Two studies made within recent years, one French and the other British, have confirmed what has already been told of the rugged paternal incubation of the Emperor's egg and have added unmistakable evidence of the fact that during the two months through which the male bird incubates the egg he eats nothing whatever, as we have seen, living apparently on his own fat and losing during the period as much as twenty pounds. What, then, of the period after hatching when the chick must be fed and the ice has not yet broken up and no seafood is available? We now have at least a partial answer to that question.

The male bird has glands in his throat which secrete a substance of the color and consistency of scrambled eggs. This apparently not only satisfies the chick but causes him to develop with surprising rapidity.

What we now know of the habits of the Emperor can be put together to explain the resourceful creature's predilection for painful propagation. In the first place it is apparent that the Antarctic summer is far too short and far too unreliable to allow normal time for the Emperor's courtship, incubation, and the develop-

ment of the chick to the point of self-reliance—which involves ability to swim and dive for food. In order to be sturdy enough to survive during the Antarctic winters the young must be well grown by January, which in fact they are, weighing at that time from twenty-five to thirty pounds. This means, since it takes two months to hatch an egg and roughly five months for the chick to attain its proper weight, that the egg must be laid in late May or early June. Although May, June, and the first half of July are dark as the ace of spades in Antarctica, the Emperor has no choice.

It is apparent then that the bird's choice of the worst possible incubating conditions is not voluntary. He may have chosen to live in the Antarctic instead of on coasts and islands farther north as his cousins do, but he has no choice but to accept the conditions which go with his habitat. It is a matter of arithmetic. For Emperor penguins, figures do not lie. These great birds would be extinct if the time clock within their amazing bodies failed to count correctly and impel them to do the right thing at the right time.

It is not so readily apparent why the male bird is elected to do the incubating. Twenty years ago it was supposed that the male and female took turns at warming the egg, the male going to the corner of the ice for a snack while the female took over. We now know that the female has no part in the actual incubation other than in the first few moments after laying. We do not know exactly why.

We do know that in early August (the date varies according to the location of the rookery) the birds which have been absent, keeping fit at the edge of the sea ice, begin returning to take over the care of the young. There is evidence that in many cases the female will seek and find her own chick but apparently she often does not. There are never enough chicks to go around and there is considerable bargain-sale fighting for possession, often causing the chicks to hide where they cannot be found and cannot take care of themselves and where they simply die of starvation and cold. Those which survive strike out on their own, riding the drifting ice to the northward, to gorge themselves on the harvest of the sea, fattening up for the cruel struggle of eventual parenthood.

There are some points in the life history of the Emperor penguin on which scientists are not yet entirely in agreement. Are they, perhaps, primitive birds which have never reached the winged state? Or are they descended from more advanced creatures, their present form and habits being merely an adaptation to environment? Are penguins an originally polar family of which the less hardy have migrated north, some as far as the Galapagos Islands, along cool ocean currents, leaving only the rugged Emperor in its ancestral home? Probably not. They are more likely an originally temperate race whose hardier members, pushing like mankind ever closer to the colder regions, have managed to achieve the ultimate in adaptation, breeding, rearing young, and surviving under conditions which no other living creature could endure.

Definite answers to these questions will, without doubt, soon be found. Whatever the answers are they can hardly make the Emperor penguin, considered from the human point of view, less than a marvel, nor render the mystery of his tenacity of life less than a miracle.

9.

The Mystery of Portugal Cove

The sea is still one of the greatest of nature's mysteries. Until the fifteenth century, it was supposed that the water and the land divided the surface of the earth about equally. We now know that exposed land exists only in a little more than a quarter of the surface of the globe, that almost three-quarters is covered by sea water at an average depth of 12,000 feet.

Anyone who took the trouble to look at television during 1970 and 1971 will not have to consult a map to be convinced that the earth's surface is mainly water. We have had the opportunity of looking at our own earth as men have for many centuries looked at the moon. We can understand why the ancients, whether they believed the planet to be flat or spherical, believed that the ocean was a great river in which the continents were set like islands, a body of water full of magic and mysteries and terrible dangers which man grew increasingly eager to master. The greater part of the ocean remained unknown until very recently, however.

Though man was able to sail upon the great waters and extend his knowledge of the land, he did not have the equipment to study the ocean's depths. There was nothing to balance the imaginative excitement with which he added to his accounts of what he saw or thought he saw in and on the sea. Until the 1870's it was supposed that living things could not exist at a greater depth than three or four thousand feet. As the area covered by water deeper than that is far greater than the total land area of the earth, it can be seen that there was plenty of room for things not known to man, and easy for them to keep out of sight.

Modern knowledge of the sea's greatest depths began one hundred years ago, when the British research ship *Challenger* set out from Portsmouth, England, on December 18, 1872, for a trip around the world. The *Challenger's* main purpose was to test and improve existing methods of sounding, or determining the depth of the sea. There had been in the first three-quarters of the nineteenth century a great furor about sea serpents and other sea monsters. The *Challenger's* mission, however, was not to look for such fabulous creatures but rather to make a study of the contours of the bottom more accurate than existing knowledge provided, and so to help in the laying and maintenance of electric communications cables which had begun to seem very important to civilization. (It should be said that they are still important, in spite of radio and television.) Up to the time when the *Challenger* set sail on her long voyage, there had been many reports, often from supposedly reliable sea captains and other travelers by water, of creatures in the distance—and sometimes fairly close by—which bore no resemblance to anything known to man.

The sea serpent idea was a perfectly natural one. People do see things at sea, but there is usually some distortion of their view of what they see, and reports made in perfectly good faith are not always particularly accurate. Up to 1872 when the *Challenger* sailed, sea serpents of several different kinds had been reported from many parts of the world's oceans. There were some that were supposed to be as much as a hundred feet long and to look like enormously exaggerated snakes with undulating bodies which moved forward in coils and waves as they swam. No one has ever found a satisfactory explanation of these serpent-like creatures although many have tried to explain them, and no actual specimen has ever been found washed ashore or taken at sea so that no scientific study of their nature has ever been made.

That a great many apparently strange creatures found on beaches and shoals were often identified as some new species was the result of the curious fact that many large inhabitants of the sea do not look in death and partial decay like the living creatures which they once were. Small whales as rotting skeletons can appear to the layman to be the carcasses of unfamiliar sea monsters. The great basking shark has, when beached and partially decayed, often been mistaken for a dead sea serpent. Many books have been written defending those who claim to have seen live sea monsters, and there is no reason to doubt that there may be such a thing as a great creature unknown to man swimming in various parts of the sea. There is lots of room to hide in the depths of the ocean where, until it was discovered that life could exist at great depths, there were believed to be serpents and the like which merely kept out of sight most of the time.

As early as the sixteenth century, Olaus Magnus wrote of a great creature found off the coast of Norway which from his description seemed to be a highly exaggerated octopus or squid. The squid and octopus were very familiar to the early inhabitants of the Atlantic and Mediterranean coasts and the smaller varieties were used as an article of diet as they are today, but no one had ever seen at close range a creature which looked anything like the one Olaus Magnus described and which was described again in the eighteenth century by Bishop Pontoppidan in his *Natural History of Norway*. The Bishop described a sea monster which came ashore on the Norwegian coast and which got itself wedged between rocks where it was observed by man and where it remained to disintegrate and disappear.

Later on in the nineteenth century, in the midst of many tales brought home by seafarers describing strange beasts, a vessel called the *Alecton* commanded by Frédéric Marie Bruyer was attacked by an unknown monster which threw its enormous tentacles over the deck of the ship and tried to pull it under—at least that is the story which the captain told in an affidavit made after his return to shore. The crew of the *Alecton* got axes and knives and chopped away at the vast tentacles which had seized the superstructure of the ship and was trying to tip it over. They succeeded in cutting off one or more of the great tentacles which fell to the deck and were examined by the crew, but the creature itself slid off into the sea and disappeared, and only the description made by the excited captain and crew enables us to wonder what it was.

It was, curiously enough, not until the decade in which the *Challenger* set forth on her voyage that there was an opportunity to conclude definitely that there was such a thing as a cephalopod (a creature like the octopus with arms coming out of its head) big enough to endanger small vessels. In 1873, some fishermen from St. John's, Newfoundland, were out in a boat about twenty feet long and four or five feet wide fishing off the coast. They were startled, when some way off shore, to be attacked by something with enormous arms which to them resembled an octopus. The great arms had huge suckers attached to them. The frantic animal

threw its arms up and out of the water, folded them over the boat, and struggled to pull the vessel under. The fishermen used their knives to hack at the tentacles which had seized the vessel and managed to cut their way loose. They returned home, shaken and terrified, with a severed arm of the great monster as a trophy.

This adventure was reported to the Reverend Moses Harvey in St. John's, who was an amateur naturalist. Harvey became very much excited at the thought that he might be the one to prove the existence of a great sea monster, in this case not a sea serpent but a veritable sea giant. He told the fishermen that he wanted a complete animal and asked them to keep their eyes open when they went out again.

When the people of that part of Newfoundland heard the story of the fishermen's adventure and of Moses Harvey's interest in it, they believed—perhaps because Harvey said he wanted a specimen of the animal to present to the Queen—that there might be a reward offered if they could find a creature of the same variety. A short while after the adventure of the fishermen, some other men from Portugal Cove, Newfoundland, were out some distance from land to investigate a seine net which they had set to catch fish. When they reached the net they saw that is was in a state of violent upheaval. This certainly was unusual—they had never seen anything like it before. As they approached the net, they could see that some great creature was caught in it and they resolved, in spite of their fear and perhaps with a possible reward in mind, to capture whatever it was. Somehow or other they got it ashore and up on the beach, where it lay spouting water with such violence that the ejected stream made great runnels in the sand. (Cephalopods of the squid variety all propel themselves by taking in water at one end and discharging it like a jet from the other end, thus moving themselves backwards through the water.)

Moses Harvey was again notified and came to see what had been captured. He was in a transport of delight, for here was an apparently complete animal never before seen. Harvey persuaded the fishermen to deliver the great bulk of the strange creature to him. He happened to have at his home an enormous vat; it is not stated just why he had it or what use he made of it but it seemed to be sufficiently large to hold all of the parts of the monster which had been brought ashore. Harvey got the remains into the vat, then filled the vessel with brine to preserve the flesh of the creature.

Fortunately Harvey had sense enough to send for a naturalist whom he knew, Addison Verrill of Connecticut, who came immediately, or as immediately as travel in those days would allow, and viewed the creature which Harvey had taken from the vat and draped over something which he referred to as a sponge bath. This was a metal frame set in a large pan in which apparently the clergyman stood when he wanted to wash himself and doused his body with water. It was a large device, plenty large enough to hold a standing man. In this peculiar contraption, at considerable sacrifice to himself since it meant that he could not take a bath, Harvey managed to drape the limbs and head of the great creature which had been brought in from the sea. His photograph taken of the animal in the sponge bath is very famous and was the first actual verification of the reality of such a monster, to which Addison Verrill, the scientist, gave the name *Architeuthis harveyi*, or *Architeuthis princeps*, which is the name by which it is known today.

This creature, the body of which was missing since it had been lost in the struggle to bring it ashore, proved when stretched out on the beach to be fifty-five feet long from tentacle to tentacle.

The head, which had been preserved, was the most remarkable feature of the whole animal. It had two great eyes as large as dinner plates with pupils and cornea very much like the human eye but terrifying in their size and apparent depth. In addition to the eyes, the creature's head was distinguished by a beak like a parrot's, only larger than an entire bird, being from four or five inches in length. The lower jaw of the beak was somewhat longer than the upper.

Here was really a sea monster and Moses Harvey was entitled to the credit for having discovered it. The minister's discovery, like all squids, large and small, belonged to that part of the animal kingdom known as mollusks, in which are also included such very different and very familiar sea inhabitants as oysters and clams. It is now known as the giant squid and is still rare, although during the decade of 1870-1880 there were a great many seen in the sea off Newfoundland, particularly on the Grand Banks where fishermen from New England and Newfoundland did their fishing, as many as fifty-five or sixty having been reported. Several were also washed ashore unstudied and it no longer was a matter of doubt that such a thing as a sea monster, if not a sea serpent, existed.

The peculiar thing is that all of these creatures were seen or washed ashore in Newfoundland in the same decade—between 1870 and 1880—the *Challenger* was at sea establishing the science of oceanography. Giant squid have rarely been seen since. Some few have been reported but nòt many. No one has been able to explain the concentration of these creatures at the time they appeared nor why they appeared in such numbers off Newfoundland. It can only be supposed that some shift in the sources of their food brought them to the coast of Newfoundland or that some submarine upheaval drove them shoreward where they are not usually found.

It is very rare to find a specimen of *Architeuthis princeps* today but they do exist. Specimens have been reported up to seventy feet in length but there are no living examples for anyone to look at. Most museums today have models of the giant squid; there is a very excellent one in the Museum of Natural History in New York City, hanging from the ceiling in the Hall of Oceanography. As has been said, Moses Harvey's find consisted of head and arms only, the creature's body having been lost in the capture. It is known, however, from other monsters taken elsewhere, that the body is from five to eight or nine feet long, as thick as a barrel, and strengthened not by bones but by an inner cartilage running down the middle of the flesh.

How such occasionally plentiful a creature can at the same time be a comparative rarity is illustrated by the work of the research vessel *Challenger*. In a voyage of three-and-a-half years, during which the ship visited every arm and corner of the world's seas, the crew apparently saw no sea monsters of any kind. In the many volumes of reports on the observations and collections made during the *Challenger's* travels, there is no mention whatever of giant squids or sea serpents of any kind.

It would be indeed wonderful if some specimen of the sea serpent, that undulating creature which has been reported so many times from the deep seas, could be found on some shore or captured in a net, but none ever has. And while it is doubtful that anyone will be so fortunate as Moses Harvey was in the case of the giant squid, to have one practically washed up on his doorstep, it is possible that some scientific verification of the existence of other forms of sea monsters will be made in the future. The sea is still a mystery and its inhabitants are still far from completely known.

For Further Reading

CHAPTER 1

Lankester, Sir E. Ray. *Monograph of the Okapi.* London: British Museum, 1910.

Smithsonian Institute Annual Report, 1901, pp. 661-666. Washington, D. C.

Stanley, Henry M. *Through the Dark Continent.* New York: Harper & Brothers, 1878.

Turnbull, Colin M. *Wayward Servants: The Two Worlds of the African Pygmies.* Garden City, New York: The Natural History Press, 1965.

CHAPTER 2

McCook, Henry C. *The Honey Ants of the Garden of the Gods, and the Occident Ants of the American Plains.* Philadelphia: J. B. Lippincott & Co., 1882.

Wheeler, William Morton. *Ants: Their Structure, Development and Behavior.* New York: Columbia University Press, 1913.

CHAPTER 3

Silver, Helenette and Walter T. *Growth and Behavior of the Coyote-like Canid of Northern New England.* Wildlife Monograph #17, October, 1969. A Publication of the Wildlife Society, Washington, D. C.

CHAPTER 4

Mershon, W. B., ed. *The Passenger Pigeon.* New York: The Outing Publishing Co., 1907.

Schorger, Ailie W. *Passenger Pigeon—Its Natural History and Extinction.* Madison: University of Wisconsin Press, 1954.

Wisconsin Society for Ornithology. *Silent Wings: A Memorial to the Passenger Pigeon.* Madison, 1947.

CHAPTER 5

New York State Fisheries, Game and Forests Commission, 4th Annual Report, pp. 193 ff. Albany, 1899.

CHAPTER 6

Emerton, J. H. *The Common Spiders of the United States.* Boston: Ginn & Co., 1902.

Fabre, Henri. *The Life of the Spider*. New York: Doubleday & Company, 1912.

Gertsch, Willis J. *American Spiders*. New York: D. Van Nostrand Company, Inc., 1949.

McCook, Henry C. *American Spiders and their Spinningwork*. 3 vols. Philadelphia, 1894.

Chapter 7

Wheeler, William Morton. *Ants: Their Structure, Development and Behavior*. New York: Columbia University Press, 1913.

———. *Social Life Among the Insects*. New York: Harcourt, Brace and Company, 1923.

Chapter 8

Stonehouse, Bernard. *The Emperor Penguin: Breeding Behaviour and Development*. Falkland Islands Dependencies Survey. Scientific Reports No. 6. London: Her Majesty's Stationery Office, 1953.

Chapter 9

Carrington, Richard. *Mermaids and Mastodons: A Book of Natural and Unnatural History*. London: The Scientific Book Guild, Beaverbrook Newspapers Limited, 1961.

Lane, Frank W. *Kingdom of the Octopus*. New York: Sheridan House, 1960.

Index

The Author

Raymond Holden is a native New Yorker with a great variety of interests. Bird classes in Central Park when he was seven or eight awakened his interest in the natural world, and for all of his life he has been a keen student of natural history. For more than twenty years, he has lived in the country, where he has maintained a bird-banding station, collected and mounted natural history specimens, and had time to explore and enjoy the world of field and forest.

His writing is marked by variety also. In the New York years, he wrote novels, mystery stories, biography, and several volumes of poetry. Since moving to New Hampshire he has also written books for young people, including *All About Famous Scientific Expeditions*, *All About Fire*, *Famous Fossil Finds*, and *The Ways of Nesting Birds*. These New Hampshire years have also seen the publication of two adult books, *The Merrimack* (in the Rivers of America Series) and *The Reminding Salt* (poetry).

He and his wife Barbara make their home in Newport, New Hampshire, where they have both been active in the cause of better libraries.

The Illustrator

Sherry Streeter is originally from Connecticut and has worked for a design studio and an advertising agency in New Haven. She now lives in New York City, working as a free-lance artist and an illustrator of children's books.

Miss Streeter holds a B.F.A. degree from Syracuse University and also studied art in Florence, Italy. Besides her work, she enjoys photography, crafts, sewing, skiing, animals, and children.